# Level 2 • Part 1
# Integrated Chinese

中文听说读写
中文聽説讀寫

## WORKBOOK Simplified and Traditional Characters

**Third Edition**

**THIRD EDITION BY**

Yuehua Liu and Tao-chung Yao
Liangyan Ge, Nyan-Ping Bi, Yaohua Shi

**ORIGINAL EDITION BY**

Yuehua Liu and Tao-chung Yao
Nyan-Ping Bi and Yaohua Shi

CHENG & TSUI COMPANY
BOSTON

Published by
Cheng & Tsui Company, Inc.
25 West Street
Boston, MA 02111-1213 USA
Fax (617) 426-3669
www.cheng-tsui.com
"Bringing Asia to the World"™


ISBN 978-0-88727-683-5


Cover Design: studioradia.com

Cover Photographs: Man with map © Getty Images; Shanghai skyline © David Pedre/iStockphoto; Building with masks © Wu Jie; Night market © Andrew Buko. Used by permission.

Interior Design: Wanda España, Wee Design

Illustrations: 洋洋兔动漫

Map of China on p. 183: base map © exxorian/iStockphoto, adapted by Mapping Specialists, Inc.

Horse image on p. 136: adapted from flickr/Kyknoord


The *Integrated Chinese* series includes books, workbooks, character workbooks, audio products, multimedia products, teacher's resources, and more. Visit **www.cheng-tsui.com** for more information on the other components of *Integrated Chinese*.


Printed in Canada.

# Contents

# Preface to the Third Edition

This workbook accompanies the third edition of *Integrated Chinese* (*IC*), Level 2 Part 1. The exercises cover the language form and the four language skills of listening, speaking, reading, and writing. They are arranged by language skill into four sections: Listening Comprehension, Speaking, Reading Comprehension, and Writing & Grammar. Within each section, exercises vary in difficulty in order to provide flexibility to suit different curricular needs.

These exercises are designed primarily for students to do outside of class, either as preparation before class or assignments after class. For instance, the listening comprehension questions based on the text of each lesson should be done when students are preparing for the lesson for the first time or before they read the text. The other exercises are for students to prepare at home, although some of them, particularly speaking exercises, can also be done in class. Unless otherwise indicated, all the exercises in the Writing and Grammar Exercises section should be done in Chinese. In general, teachers should assign the exercises at their discretion; they should not feel pressured into using all of them and should feel free to use them out of sequence, if appropriate. Moreover, teachers can complement this workbook with their own exercises.

We have made several improvements and added a number of new features in the third edition of the workbook.

## Three Modes of Communication

Our exercises cover the three modes of communication—interpretive, interpersonal, and presentational—as explained in "Standards for Foreign Language Learning in the 21st Century." We have labeled the exercises as interpretive, interpersonal, or presentational wherever applicable.

## Listening Rejoinders

To help students develop interpersonal skills, we have added a rejoinder to each lesson. The rejoinders are designed to improve students' ability to listen and respond to questions or remarks logically and meaningfully.

## Character and Word Building Exercises

While training students to work on their proficiency at the sentence and paragraph-length levels, we realized there was a need to help students solidify their foundation in character recognition and word association. We have thus added character and word building exercises to each lesson.

# New Reading Exercises

To help students understand how their newly acquired vocabulary and grammatical structures function in meaningful contexts and, at the same time, to avoid overwhelming students with extra materials containing words they haven't learned, we have added newly composed reading exercises and deleted the ancient Chinese parables that were included in previous editions. These parables, however, are now available online at PeerSource, **my.cheng-tsui.com**. Students should be encouraged to use them as supplementary reading materials with the help of a dictionary.

# More Authentic Materials

To build a bridge between the pedagogical materials used in the classroom and the materials that students will encounter in the target language environment, we have added more authentic materials such as signs, posters, advertisements, and other documents in the exercises for all lessons.

# New Illustrations

To make the exercises more interesting and appealing, we have added many illustrations to the exercises. These visual images increase the variety of exercise types, and also encourage students to answer questions directly in Chinese without going through the translation process.

# Contextualized Grammar Exercises and Task-Oriented Assignments

The ultimate goal of learning any language is to be able to communicate in that language. With this goal in mind, we pay equal attention to language form and language function, and have created task-based exercises to train students to handle real-life situations using the language accurately and appropriately. We have rewritten many items, especially in the translation section, to provide linguistic context and to reflect the language used in real life.

# Learner-Centered Tasks

We believe that the exercises in the workbook should not only integrate the content of the textbook, but also relate to student life. We include exercises that simulate daily life with topics and themes that students can easily relate to. We hope these exercises will actively engage students in the subject matter and keep them interested in the language-learning process. Since the world is constantly changing, we also have tried to add exercises that will train students to meet the needs of today's world, such as writing e-mail messages in Chinese.

# Storytelling Exercises

To coach students to describe what they see and use their language skills to construct narratives, we have added one storytelling exercise to each lesson. This exercise is designed to help students develop skills for organizing ideas and presenting them in a coherent manner. It also provides practice in using transitional elements and cohesive devices to make the story progress smoothly and logically. This exercise is suitable for either speaking or writing. The teacher can ask students to submit the story as a written exercise and/or ask them to make an oral presentation in class.

## New Review Exercises

At the end of every five lessons, a cumulative review unit is available to those students who wish to do a periodic progress check. These units are flexible, short, and useful as a review tool. They include exercises that reinforce a variety of language skills, from practicing pronunciation to recalling vocabulary and writing cohesive narratives. Since the review units do not introduce any new learning topics, they can be included in the teaching plan at the teacher's discretion.

## Acknowledgments

We would like to take this opportunity to thank all those who have given us feedback in the past, and extend our sincere gratitude to Professor Zheng-sheng Zhang of San Diego State University and to Ms. Kristen Wanner for their invaluable editorial comments and to Ms. Laurel Damashek at Cheng & Tsui for her support throughout the editorial and production process. We welcome your comments and feedback; please send any observations or suggestions to **editor@cheng-tsui.com.**

# Preface to the Second Edition

In designing the Level Two workbook exercises for *Integrated Chinese*, we strove to give equal emphasis to students' listening, speaking, reading, and writing skills. There are different difficulty levels in order to provide variety and flexibility to suit different curriculum needs. Teachers can assign the exercises at their discretion; they need not feel pressure to use all of them. If appropriate, teachers can use them out of sequence. Moreover, teachers can supplement this workbook with their own exercises.

## What's New in the Second Edition

Thanks to all those who have used *Integrated Chinese* and given us the benefit of their suggestions and comments, we have been able to produce a second edition that includes the following improvements.

**Level 2 workbook offers full text in simplified and traditional characters.** The original workbook, although geared toward both traditional-and simplified-character learners, contained sections in which only the traditional characters were given. This was of course problematic for students who were principally interested in learning simplified characters. This difficulty has been resolved in the new edition, as we now provide both traditional and simplified characters for every Chinese sentence. The only exception is the authentic materials. All authentic materials used in the workbook are presented in their original characters to preserve their authenticity. An appendix containing alternate character versions is provided as a learning tool for those interested in reading both forms.

The workbook's **exercises have been revised extensively** to recycle vocabulary learned and to provide a contextualized language environment. New and different varieties of exercises have been added, and more authentic materials are included. Teachers can choose exercises that best suit their needs. When words that have not been taught are used in the exercises, glosses have been provided.

A **Chinese-English vocabulary index** and an **English-Chinese vocabulary index** have been added to the workbook. The indices contain new vocabulary words that are glossed in the exercises. (See the textbook indices for vocabulary words appearing in the lessons.)

In addition to written instructions, **new illustrations and photos** provide the reader with visual interest, linguistic clues, and relevant cultural information.

Typographical errors present in the first edition have been corrected, and the content has been carefully edited to ensure accuracy and minimize errors.

# How to Use This Workbook

## Listening Comprehension

All too often listening comprehension is sacrificed in a formal classroom setting because of time constraints. Students tend to focus their time and energy on the mastery of a few grammar points, rather than on developing strong listening skills. This workbook tries to remedy this imbalance by including a substantial number of listening comprehension exercises. There are two categories of listening exercises; both can be done on the students' own time or in the classroom. In either case, it is important to have the instructor review the students' answers for accuracy.

The first category of listening exercises, which is at the beginning of each listening section, is based on the text of each lesson. For the exercises to be meaningful, students should first study the vocabulary list, and then listen to the recordings of the texts. The questions are provided to help students' aural understanding of the texts.

The second category of listening exercises consists of an audio CD recording of two or more mini-dialogues or narratives. These exercises are designed to give students extra practice on the vocabulary and grammar points introduced in the lesson. Some of the exercises, especially ones that ask students to choose among several possible answers, are significantly more difficult than others. These exercises should be assigned toward the end of the lesson, when the students have become familiar with the content of the lesson.

## Speaking Exercises

Here, too, there are two types of exercises. They are designed for different levels of proficiency within each lesson and should be assigned at the appropriate time.

To help students apply their newly acquired vocabulary and grammatical understanding to meaningful communication, we first ask them questions related to the dialogues and narratives, and then ask them questions related to their own lives. These questions require one-or two-sentence answers. By stringing together short questions and answers, students can construct their own mini-dialogues, practice in pairs, or take turns asking or answering questions.

Once they have gained some confidence, students can progress to the more difficult questions, where they are invited to express opinions on a number of topics. Typically, these questions are abstract, so they gradually teach students to express their opinions in longer conversations. As the school year progresses, these types of questions should take up more class discussion time. Because this second type of speaking exercise is quite challenging, it should be attempted only **after** students are well grounded in the grammar and vocabulary of a particular lesson. Usually, this occurs not immediately after students have completed the first part of the speaking exercises.

## Reading Comprehension

There are three types of reading exercises in the workbook: 1) short passages incorporating new vocabulary and grammatical structures from the lesson; 2) authentic materials such as advertisements, personal ads, and short news articles (some slightly modified); and 3) ancient Chinese parables. The sequence generally reflects the degree of difficulty of the materials, with the short passages being the most straightforward. The authentic materials are included not only because of their pedagogical value but also for their sociological interest. The various parables, on the other hand, originate from classical "wisdom texts" and have long been familiar set phrases. The variety of the readings is a way to bring culture—contemporary and ancient—into language learning while also allowing flexibility to the instructor. Occasionally, words that may be unfamiliar to some students appear in the reading passages, and these words are not glossed. But they will not prevent students from completing the tasks assigned successfully. Students are encouraged to guess the meaning of these words from the context of the reading passage.

## Writing and Grammar Exercises

### *Grammar and Usage*

These drills and exercises are designed to solidify students' grasp of important grammar points. Through brief exchanges, students answer questions using specific grammatical forms, or are given sentences to complete. These exercises are not simple mechanical drills since their completion depends on students correctly understanding the contextual clues.

In the second half of the Level 2 textbook, students are introduced to increasingly sophisticated and abstract vocabulary. Corresponding exercises in this workbook help them to grasp the nuances of new words. For example, synonyms are a source of great difficulty; so exercises are provided to help students distinguish them.

### *Translation*

Translation has been a tool for language teaching throughout the ages, and positive student feedback confirms our belief that it continues to play an important role. The exercises we have devised serve to reinforce two primary areas: one, to help students use specific grammatical structures in their speech; and two, to allow students to build their ever-increasing vocabulary. Ultimately, our hope is that this dual-pronged approach will enable students to understand that it takes more than just literal translation to convey an idea in a foreign language.

### *Writing Practice*

This is the culmination of the written exercises, and it is where students learn to express themselves in writing. Many of the topics overlap with those used in oral practice. We expect that students will find it easier to put in writing what they have already learned to express orally.

# Acknowledgments

Since publication of the first edition of *Integrated Chinese*, in 1997, many teachers and students have given us helpful comments and suggestions. We cannot list all of these individuals here, but we would like to reiterate our genuine appreciation for their help. We do wish to recognize the following individuals who have made recent contributions to the *Integrated Chinese* revision. We are indebted to Tim Richardson, Jeffrey Hayden, Ying Wang, and Xianmin Liu for field-testing the new edition and sending us their comments and corrections. We would also like to thank Chengzhi Chu for letting us try out his "Chinese TA," a computer program designed for Chinese teachers to create and edit teaching materials. This software saved us many hours of work during the revision. Last, but not least, we want to thank James Dew for his superb, professional editorial job, which enhanced both the content and the style of the new edition. We are also grateful to our editors at Cheng & Tsui, Sandra Korinchak and Kristen Wanner, for their painstaking work throughout the editing and production process. Naturally, the authors assume full responsibility for the content.

As much as we would like to eradicate all errors in the new edition, some will undoubtedly remain, so please continue to send your comments and corrections to **editor@cheng-tsui.com**, and accept our sincere thanks for your help.

第一課　　開學

第一课　　开学

## I. Listening Comprehension

### A. Textbook Content (INTERPRETIVE)

Listen to the recording for the Textbook and answer the questions in English.

**1.** What year in school is Zhang Tianming?

_____

**2.** How did Zhang Tianming get to campus?

_____

**3.** Who is Ke Lin?

_____

**4.** Where does Ke Lin live?

_____

**5.** What does Ke Lin offer to do for Zhang Tianming?

_____

_____

**6.** What happened to Zhang Tianming's computer?

_____

### B. Workbook Dialogue (INTERPRETIVE)

Listen to the recording for the Workbook and answer the questions.

Questions (True/False):

( )　**1.** The dialogue takes place in front of a dorm for first-year students.

( )　**2.** The man knows the campus very well because he is a senior at the university.

( )　**3.** The woman was on an airplane earlier today.

( )　**4.** The dorm the man lives in has been a returning students' dorm for years.

( )　**5.** The taxi driver has dropped the woman off in the wrong place.

( )　**6.** The man's dorm is on the west side of the dorm for first-year students.

## C. Workbook Narratives

1. Listen to the recording for the Workbook and answer the questions in English. (INTERPRETIVE)

   **a.** What does "zhù xiào" mean?

   **b.** What is a "shìyǒu"? What is a "tóngwū"?

2. Listen to the recording for the Workbook and answer the questions in English. (INTERPRETIVE)

   **a.** Why does Little Wang want to move out of his dorm?

   **b.** What is good about Little Wang's new place?

   **c.** Do you think Little Wang will live at his new place alone? Why or why not?

3. After listening to the recording for the Workbook, fill out Little Zhang's daily schedule in Chinese, and answer the questions that follow in English. (INTERPRETIVE AND PRESENTATIONAL)

---

### LITTLE ZHANG'S DAILY SCHEDULE

_____

_____

_____

_____

_____

_____

_____

_____

_____

_____

Questions:

    **a.** How long does Little Zhang listen to the audio recording every day?

    **b.** How many classes does Little Zhang have every day?

    **c.** Where does Little Zhang access the internet?

**4.** Write the name in Chinese characters after you listen to the recording. (INTERPRETIVE AND PRESENTATIONAL)

    **a.** _____

    **b.** _____

### D. Workbook Listening Rejoinder (INTERPERSONAL)

In this section, you will hear two people talking. After hearing the first speaker, select the best from the four possible responses given by the second speaker.

_____

## II. Speaking Exercises

**A.** In order to get to know your Chinese language partner/classmate better, find out and report the following information in Chinese. Use Chinese when you interview your partner/classmate. (INTERPERSONAL)

1. What's his or her name?

2. Where is he or she from?

3. Where was he or she born?

4. Where did he or she grow up?

5. Is he or she a college freshman?

6. Does he or she live on or off campus? Does he or she like where he or she lives? Why or why not?

7. How long has he or she been studying Chinese?

8. How does he or she write her/his Chinese name if he or she has one?

**B.** Practice asking and answering the following questions. (INTERPERSONAL)

1. 你是在什麼地方出生的？
   你是在什么地方出生的？

2. 你是在什麼地方長大的？
   你是在什么地方长大的？

3. 你今天是幾點到的教室？
   你今天是几点到的教室？

4. 你今天是怎麼來的學校？走路，開車，還是坐公共汽車？
   你今天是怎么来的学校？走路，开车，还是坐公共汽车？

5. 學校是幾號開學的？
   学校是几号开学的？

**6.** 你住校內還是住校外？

你住校内还是住校外？

**7.** 要是你有錢，你想搬到什麼地方去住？為什麼？

要是你有钱，你想搬到什么地方去住？为什么？

**C.** Practice speaking on the following topics. (PRESENTATIONAL)

**1.** 請你介紹一下你自己。

请你介绍一下你自己。

**2.** 請你談一談你上大學/高中的第一天在學校都做了些什麼。

请你谈一谈你上大学/高中的第一天在学校都做了些什么。

**3.** 你覺得住在學校宿舍好，還是住在校外好？為什麼？

你觉得住在学校宿舍好，还是住在校外好？为什么？

## III. Reading Comprehension

### A. Building Words

Complete this section by writing the characters, the *pinyin*, and the English equivalent of each new word formed. Guess the meaning before you use a dictionary to confirm.

**1.** "衛生間" 的 "衛生" + "一張紙" 的 "紙"

"卫生间" 的 "卫生" + "一张纸" 的 "纸"

→ _____ _____ _____

       new word    *pinyin*    English

**2.** "幫忙" 的 "幫" + "手"

"帮忙" 的 "帮" + "手"

→ _____ _____ _____

**3.** "學校" 的 "校" + "公園" 的 "園"

"学校" 的 "校" + "公园" 的 "园"

→ _____ _____ _____

**4.** "吃壞肚子" 的 "壞" + "好處" 的 "處"

"吃坏肚子" 的 "坏" + "好处" 的 "处"

→ _____ _____ _____

**B.** Read the conversation and answer the questions. (INTERPRETIVE)

(TRADITIONAL)

林明： 哎，王新！你怎麼又搬家了？你上個學期剛剛從校內搬到校外，現在又要搬回學校宿舍了？

王新： 住在宿舍的時候覺得房租太貴，而且不自由。可是住在校外很不方便。上個星期三早上我考試又去晚了，覺得還是搬回宿舍好，所以就搬回來了。

林明： 你不會在學校宿舍住兩個月，又想搬到校外去吧？

王新： 說真的，平時住在宿舍覺得又方便又安全，可是一到週末我還是會想起住在校外的好處：房租便宜得多，而且很自由。

林明： 我有個好辦法。你可以租兩套房子，一套在校內，一套在校外。你星期一到星期五住在校內，一到週末就住到校外去。這樣你會覺得又方便又安全，而且自由。

王新： 你這個辦法真有意思。要是我有錢，那真是個好辦法。

(SIMPLIFIED)

林明： 哎，王新！你怎么又搬家了？你上个学期刚刚从校内搬到校外，现在又要搬回学校宿舍了？

王新： 住在宿舍的时候觉得房租太贵，而且不自由。可是住在校外很不方便。上个星期三早上我考试又去晚了，觉得还是搬回宿舍好，所以就搬回来了。

林明： 你不会在学校宿舍住两个月，又想搬到校外去吧？

王新： 说真的，平时住在宿舍觉得又方便又安全，可是一到周末我还是会想起住在校外的好处：房租便宜得多，而且很自由。

林明：　我有个好办法。你可以租两套房子，一套在校内，一套在校外。你星期一到星期五住在校内，一到周末就住到校外去。这样你会觉得又方便又安全，而且自由。

王新：　你这个办法真有意思。要是我有钱，那真是个好办法。

Questions (True/False)

( )  **1.**  Wang Xin has been living in the student dorm for a semester.

( )  **2.**  Lin Ming thinks Wang Xin has moved too many times.

( )  **3.**  One of the reasons that Wang Xin moved out of the dorm was that it was too expensive.

( )  **4.**  Wang Xin had never been late for his examinations until last Wednesday.

( )  **5.**  It was not easy for Wang Xin to make the decision to move one more time.

( )  **6.**  Wang Xin has already made the decision to move again in two months.

( )  **7.**  Lin Ming thinks Wang Xin is never sure about where he should live.

( )  **8.**  According to Wang Xin, it is much less expensive to live off campus.

( )  **9.**  If Wang Xin follows Lin Ming's suggestion, he will be able to save money.

**C.** Review Zhang Tianming's schedule and complete the subsequent passage accordingly.
(INTERPRETIVE)

| | | |
|---|---|---|
| 早上 | 起床<br>吃早飯<br>上中文課<br>上電腦課<br>上網 | 起床<br>吃早饭<br>上中文课<br>上电脑课<br>上网 |
| 下午 | 吃午飯<br>上音樂課<br>打球<br>回宿舍 | 吃午饭<br>上音乐课<br>打球<br>回宿舍 |
| 晚上 | 吃晚飯<br>做功課<br>看電視<br>睡覺 | 吃晚饭<br>做功课<br>看电视<br>睡觉 |

(TRADITIONAL)

　　張天明今天早上＿＿＿＿＿以後，很快地吃了點兒早飯，就去上中文課。＿＿＿＿＿，沒能休息，就去上電腦課。＿＿＿＿＿，他到圖書館去＿＿＿＿＿。吃午飯的時候，柯林坐在他的旁邊。柯林說：“我今天有四節課，已經上了三節了，你呢？”小張回答說：“我＿＿＿＿＿，還有一節音樂課。”下午回宿舍前，張天明跟朋友去＿＿＿＿＿。＿＿＿＿＿，才回宿舍吃晚飯。張天明今天的功課不多，＿＿＿＿＿一個鐘頭就＿＿＿＿＿。然後，＿＿＿＿＿半個鐘頭的電視，就上床睡覺了。

(SIMPLIFIED)

　　张天明今天早上_____以后，很快地吃了点儿早饭，就去上中文课。_____，没能休息，就去上电脑课。_____，他到图书馆去_____。吃午饭的时候，柯林坐在他的旁边。柯林说："我今天有四节课，已经上了三节了，你呢？"小张回答说："我_____，还有一节音乐课。"下午回宿舍前，张天明跟朋友去_____。_____，才回宿舍吃晚饭。张天明今天的功课不多，_____一个钟头就_____。然后，_____半个钟头的电视，就上床睡觉了。

**D.** Take a look at this business card and answer the questions in Chinese. (INTERPRETIVE AND PRESENTATIONAL)

Questions:

1. 這個人姓什麼？怎麼介紹他的姓？
   这个人姓什么？怎么介绍他的姓？

_____

2. 他在哪一個城市工作？
   他在哪一个城市工作？

_____

3. 他是做什麼的？老師，醫生，還是律師？
   他是做什么的？老师，医生，还是律师？

_____

# IV. Writing and Grammar Exercises

## A. Building Characters

Form a character by combining the given components as indicated. Then write a word, a phrase, or a short sentence in which that character appears.

1. 左邊一個"車"，右邊一個"兩"，
   左边一个"车"，右边一个"两"，
   是 _____ 的 _____ 。

2. 上邊一個"少"，下邊一個"目"，
   上边一个"少"，下边一个"目"，
   是 _____ 的 _____ 。

3. 左邊一個"弓"，右邊一個"長"，
   左边一个"弓"，右边一个"长"，
   是 _____ 的 _____ 。

4. 左邊一個"木"，右邊一個"可"，
   左边一个"木"，右边一个"可"，
   是 _____ 的 _____ 。

**B.** Answer the following questions in Chinese based on your own situation. (INTERPERSONAL)

1. **A:** 學校開學幾天了？

   学校开学几天了？

   **B:** _____ ○

2. **A:** 你學中文學了幾個學期了？

   你学中文学了几个学期了？

   **B:** _____ ○

3. **A:** 每天吃完晚飯以後，你做什麼？

   每天吃完晚饭以后，你做什么？

   **B:** _____ ○

**C.** Answer the following questions based on your own situation. (INTERPERSONAL)

1. **A:** 你今天是幾點起的床？

   你今天是几点起的床？

   **B:** _____ ○

2. **A:** 你今天是幾點去上課的？

   你今天是几点去上课的？

   **B:** _____ ○

3. **A:** 你今天是怎麼去上課的？

   你今天是怎么去上课的？

   **B:** _____ ○

4. **A:** 你的電腦是在哪兒買的？什麼時候買的？

   你的电脑是在哪儿买的？什么时候买的？

   **B:** _____ ○

**D.** Answer the following questions in Chinese based on your own situation. (INTERPERSONAL)

**1. A:** 你這個學期除了上中文課以外，還上什麼課？
你这个学期除了上中文课以外，还上什么课？

**B:** _____ 。

**2. A:** 你除了會説中文以外，還會説什麼外國話？
你除了会说中文以外，还会说什么外国话？

**B:** _____ 。

**3. A:** 你的房間除了床以外，還有什麼傢具？
你的房间除了床以外，还有什么家具？

**B:** _____ 。

**4. A:** 這個週末除了學習、做功課以外，你還打算做什麼？
这个周末除了学习、做功课以外，你还打算做什么？

**B:** _____ 。

**E.** Let's get to know Ke Lin. Using the 除了…以外 structure, answer the questions based on the information given. (INTERPRETIVE AND PRESENTATIONAL)

EXAMPLE:

| 星期一 | 星期二 | 星期三 | 星期四 | 星期五 | 星期六 | 星期日 |
|--------|--------|--------|--------|--------|--------|--------|
| X | X | ✓ | ✓ | ✓ | ✓ | ✓ |

**A:** 柯林星期幾有空？
柯林星期几有空？

→ **B:** 柯林除了星期一、星期二以外，別的時間都有空。
柯林除了星期一、星期二以外，别的时间都有空。

**1.**

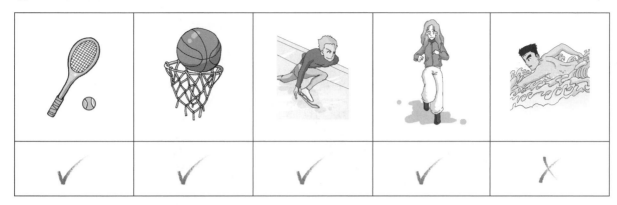

A: 柯林喜歡什麼運動?
柯林喜欢什么运动?

B: _____ 。

**2.**

| Beijing | London | New York | Tokyo | Paris | Sydney |
|---------|--------|----------|-------|-------|--------|
| X | ✓ | ✓ | ✓ | ✓ | ✓ |

A: 柯林去過哪些城市?
柯林去过哪些城市?

B: _____ 。

**3.**

| ☒ | ✓ | ✗ | ✗ | ✗ |
|---|---|---|---|---|

A: 柯林喜歡喝什麼飲料?
柯林喜欢喝什么饮料?

B: _____ 。

**F.** Answer the questions and then explain why based on your own situation or the Lesson 1 text.
(INTERPERSONAL)

EXAMPLE:

> **A:** 張天明為什麼住在學校宿舍裏？
>
> 张天明为什么住在学校宿舍里？
>
> **B:** <u>因為可以適應學校生活，再說上課也方便</u>。
>
> **B:** <u>因为可以适应学校生活，再说上课也方便</u>。

**1. A:** 你為什麼學中文？

你为什么学中文？

**B:** _____

**2. A:** 你為什麼上這個學校？

你为什么上这个学校？

**B:** _____

**3. A:** 柯林為什麼住在校外？

柯林为什么住在校外？

**B:** _____

**G.** Complete the following exchanges using 不見得/不见得.

EXAMPLE:

> **A:** 他父母是中國人，雖然他生在美國，但是學中文應該很容易吧？
>
> 他父母是中国人，虽然他生在美国，但是学中文应该很容易吧？
>
> **B:** <u>在美國長大的中國孩子，學中文不見得容易</u>。
>
> <u>在美国长大的中国孩子，学中文不见得容易</u>。

**1. A:** 這個宿舍又小又貴。我真想搬出去住，省點兒錢。

这个宿舍又小又贵。我真想搬出去住，省点儿钱。

**B:** 很多校外的房子也很小很貴，_____。

很多校外的房子也很小很贵，_____。

2.A: 你們這個宿舍很安靜，下個學期我打算搬進來。

你们这个宿舍很安静，下个学期我打算搬进来。

B: 這個宿舍房間不多，好像都有人住，＿＿＿＿＿＿＿＿＿。

这个宿舍房间不多，好像都有人住，＿＿＿＿＿＿＿＿＿。

3.A: 他是老生，我們有什麼事都可以去問他。

他是老生，我们有什么事都可以去问他。

B: 他只比我們早來一年，＿＿＿＿＿＿＿＿＿＿＿＿＿＿。

他只比我们早来一年，＿＿＿＿＿＿＿＿＿＿＿＿＿＿。

**H.** Zhang Tianming can be a scatterbrain. Based on the illustrations given, imagine what he would say when he realizes he has left something behind. (PRESENTATIONAL)

EXAMPLE:

→ <u>糟糕，我把電腦拉在出租車上了</u>。

<u>糟糕，我把电脑拉在出租车上了</u>。

1. ＿＿＿＿＿＿＿＿＿＿＿＿＿＿＿＿＿＿＿＿＿＿＿＿＿＿＿。

2. ＿＿＿＿＿＿＿＿＿＿＿＿＿＿＿＿＿＿＿＿＿＿＿＿＿＿＿。

3. ＿＿＿＿＿＿＿＿＿＿＿＿＿＿＿＿＿＿＿＿＿＿＿＿＿＿＿。

**I.** Fill in the blanks with the words or phrases given. (INTERPRETIVE)

(TRADITIONAL)

> **1.**除了　　**2.**以外　　**3.**因為　　**4.**再說

王健是在北京出生，在北京長大的。高中畢業以後，他父母就叫他到這個大學來留學。王健問爸爸為什麼要來這個大學？爸爸說：“_____這個大學很有名，老師很好。_____學校有名、老師好_____，聽說從這個學校畢業的學生找到工作也容易。_____你阿姨就住在這個城市，週末你可以去阿姨家吃中國飯，就不會很想家，能快一點適應在美國的生活。”

(SIMPLIFIED)

> **1.**除了　　**2.**以外　　**3.**因为　　**4.**再说

王健是在北京出生，在北京长大的。高中毕业以后，他父母就叫他到这个大学来留学。王健问爸爸为什么要来这个大学？爸爸说：“_____这个大学很有名，老师很好。_____学校有名、老师好_____，听说从这个学校毕业的学生找到工作也容易。_____你阿姨就住在这个城市，周末你可以去阿姨家吃中国饭，就不会很想家，能快一点适应在美国的生活。”

Now answer the following question using 第一…，第二…，第三…：

王健的爸爸為什麼叫他來這個大學學習？
王健的爸爸为什么叫他来这个大学学习？

**J.** Translate the following exchanges into Chinese. (PRESENTATIONAL)

    **1. A:** When will school start?

       **B:** Next Wednesday.

_____

_____

    **2. A:** What time did you get home yesterday?

       **B:** I got home at 10:30 p.m.

_____

_____

    **3. A:** Did you go to New York by plane or by car?

       **B:** I went by car.

_____

_____

    **4. A:** Living in the dormitory is very convenient.

       **B:** But it doesn't necessarily save you money.

_____

_____

**K.** Translate the following passages into Chinese. (PRESENTATIONAL)

    **1.** That first-year student was born in China, but raised in America. Yesterday I helped her move into her dorm. Her parents want her to live in the dorm to get used to college life, but she feels that living in the dorm is too restrictive and she wants to live off campus next semester.

_____

_____

_____

_____

_____

**2.** Zhang Tianming got to know a new friend this morning. His name is Ke Lin. Zhang Tianming met Ke Lin in the dorm. There were many people in the dorm, and except for Ke Lin, Zhang Tianming didn't know anyone else. Ke Lin helped Zhang Tianming move his stuff. After helping him move, Ke Lin said to Zhang Tianming, "If you need any help, call me."

_____

_____

_____

_____

_____

**3.** Little Zhang is from China. He just moved to the United States last year. He has been living in California for more than a year, yet he still hasn't adapted to life in America. He thinks that it's really inconvenient to live in America without a car. He often has to ask others to take him shopping. Next semester he would like to buy a car and help other new students from China.

_____

_____

_____

_____

_____

**L.** Describe your first day in college/high school. Include information such as when and how you got to the campus, whether you liked your living quarters and why, and which classmates or dorm-mates you met that day. (PRESENTATIONAL)

## M. Storytelling (PRESENTATIONAL)

Write a story in Chinese based on the four cartoons below. Make sure that your story has a beginning, a middle, and an end. Also make sure that the transition from one picture to the next is smooth and logical.

1

2

3

4

第二課　　宿舍

第二課　　宿舍

# I. Listening Comprehension

## A. Textbook Content (INTERPRETIVE)

Listen to the recording for the Textbook and answer the questions in English.

**1.** Who moved in first, Zhang Tianming or his roommate?

_____

**2.** What furniture do Zhang Tianming and his roommate both have?

_____

**3.** Is their dorm close to a main street?

_____

**4.** What are the advantages of living in the dorm?

_____

**5.** What are the disadvantages of living in the dorm?

_____

## B. Workbook Dialogue (INTERPRETIVE)

Listen to the recording for the Workbook and answer the questions.

Questions (True/False):

( )　**1.** Daming's building is located in a quiet environment.

( )　**2.** Daming does not like his room in the dorm.

( )　**3.** Daming's friend lives in the same dorm but on a different floor.

( )　**4.** Daming will most likely continue to live in the dorm for the rest of the semester.

Questions (Multiple Choice):

( ) **5.** During which time slot is Daming's room quietest?

    **a.** 1:00 p.m. – 4:00 p.m.

    **b.** 4:00 p.m. – 7:00 p.m.

    **c.** 7:00 p.m. – 10:00 p.m.

( ) **6.** According to Daming, what is the main source of the noise?

    **a.** over one hundred students who live on the same floor

    **b.** traffic on the major streets outside

    **c.** one of the dryers in the laundry room

## C. Workbook Narratives

**1.** Write the character based on what you hear on the recording. (INTERPRETIVE AND PRESENTATIONAL)

    **a.** _____

    **b.** _____

**2.** Listen to the recording and answer the following questions in English. (INTERPRETIVE)

    **a.** How many pieces of furniture are there in the room, and what are they?

    _____

    **b.** Does the narrator have to walk far to his classes?

    _____

    **c.** What does the narrator like about his room?

    _____

    **d.** What is the room's only shortcoming?

    _____

**3.** Draw a picture of Little Li's room based on the recording and answer in Chinese the question you hear at the end of the recording.

Answer: _____

### D. Workbook Listening Rejoinder (INTERPERSONAL)

In this section, you will hear two people talking. After hearing the first speaker, select the best from the four possible responses given by the second speaker.

_____

## II. Speaking Exercises

**A.** Practice asking and answering the following questions. (INTERPERSONAL)

**1.** 你的房間有什麼傢具？
你的房间有什么家具？

**2.** 你的書桌上擺著一些什麼東西？
你的书桌上摆着一些什么东西？

**3.** 你住的地方離學校哪一棟樓最近？
你住的地方离学校哪一栋楼最近？

**4.** 你去過的中國餐館，哪一家的菜最地道？
你去过的中国餐馆，哪一家的菜最地道？

**B.** Practice speaking on the following topics. (INTERPERSONAL)

**1.** 你的房間（我現在住在…）
你的房间（我现在住在…）

**2.** 你喜歡什麼樣的房間？
你喜欢什么样的房间？

**C.** Describe this room in detail. (PRESENTATIONAL)

## III. Reading Comprehension

### A. Building Words

Complete this section by writing the characters, the *pinyin*, and the English equivalent of each new word formed. Guess the meaning before you use a dictionary to confirm.

**1.** "商店" 的 "商" + "日用品" 的 "品"

→ ＿＿＿＿＿ ＿＿＿＿＿ ＿＿＿＿＿

　　　　new word　　*pinyin*　　English

**2.** "出去玩" 的 "玩" + "文具" 的 "具"

→ ＿＿＿＿＿ ＿＿＿＿＿ ＿＿＿＿＿

**3.** "掛衣服" 的 "掛" + "號碼" 的 "號"
"挂衣服" 的 "挂" + "号码" 的 "号"

→ ＿＿＿＿＿ ＿＿＿＿＿ ＿＿＿＿＿

**4.** "同屋" 的 "同" + "什麼事" 的 "事"
"同屋" 的 "同" + "什么事" 的 "事"

→ ＿＿＿＿＿ ＿＿＿＿＿ ＿＿＿＿＿

**5.** "地方" 的 "地" + "毯子" 的 "毯"

→ ＿＿＿＿＿ ＿＿＿＿＿ ＿＿＿＿＿

**B.** The following excerpt is part of a conversation between a landlord and a potential tenant. Read it and answer the questions in English. (INTERPRETIVE)

A: 對不起，請問，房間裏有空調嗎？
A: 对不起，请问，房间里有空调吗？
B: 沒有。這兒一般不熱。
B: 没有。这儿一般不热。
A: 衛生間大不大？
A: 卫生间大不大？
B: 一個人用，沒問題。
B: 一个人用，没问题。

**A:** 這棟樓舊不舊？

**A:** 这栋楼旧不旧？

**B:** 不是很舊，二十幾年。

**B:** 不是很旧，二十几年。

**A:** 離馬路近嗎？

**A:** 离马路近吗？

**B:** 很遠。這兒很安靜。

**B:** 很远。这儿很安静。

**A:** 有沒有洗衣機和烘乾機？

**A:** 有没有洗衣机和烘干机？

**B:** 沒有，可是離洗衣服的地方不遠。

**B:** 没有，可是离洗衣服的地方不远。

**A:** 我不喜歡做飯，附近有飯館兒嗎？

**A:** 我不喜欢做饭，附近有饭馆儿吗？

**B:** 有，旁邊有一家很地道的中國飯館。

**B:** 有，旁边有一家很地道的中国饭馆。

**A:** 房租多少錢？

**A:** 房租多少钱？

**B:** 每個月四百塊。

**B:** 每个月四百块。

**1.** Would you rent this apartment?

**2.** Explain your decision by commenting briefly on the following things:

air conditioning _____

size of bathroom _____

age of building _____

noise level _____

laundry facilities _____

restaurants _____

rent _____

**C.** Read the passage and answer the questions in English. (INTERPRETIVE)

(TRADITIONAL)

在中國，學生高中畢業以後都得考試才能上大學。考試考得好，就上好一點的大學，考得不太好，就上一般的大學。如果考試考得很不好，就不能上大學。很多大學新生一進學校，就已經知道自己的專業是什麼了，要是不喜歡，也可以換專業。但是換專業，還是得考試。

(SIMPLIFIED)

在中国，学生高中毕业以后都得考试才能上大学。考试考得好，就上好一点的大学，考得不太好，就上一般的大学。如果考试考得很不好，就不能上大学。很多大学新生一进学校，就已经知道自己的专业是什么了，要是不喜欢，也可以换专业。但是换专业，还是得考试。

Questions

**1.** How is the college admissions process in China similar to and different from that in the United States?

_____

**2.** Generally speaking, when do Chinese college students decide what to major in?

_____

**3.** If a Chinese college student doesn't like her major, what can she do?

_____

**D.** Draw a picture and answer the true/false questions after reading the following passage. (INTERPRETIVE)

(TRADITIONAL)

小高的新家有兩層樓。樓上有三個房間。左邊的房間是小高的書房。書房中間是一張很大的書桌，書桌後邊是兩個又高又大的書架。中間的房間是廁所。廁所的右邊是小高的臥室，臥室中間放著一張床，床旁邊擺著一個衣櫃。樓下有客廳，餐廳、廚房和洗衣房。洗衣房在右邊，裏邊有烘乾機和洗衣機。洗衣房的旁邊是餐廳和廚房，再過去才是客廳。小高站在門外，看著自己的新家，非常高興。

(SIMPLIFIED)

　　小高的新家有两层楼。楼上有三个房间。左边的房间是小高的书房。书房中间是一张很大的书桌，书桌后边是两个又高又大的书架。中间的房间是厕所。厕所的右边是小高的卧室，卧室中间放着一张床，床旁边摆着一个衣柜。楼下有客厅，餐厅、厨房和洗衣房。洗衣房在右边，里边有烘干机和洗衣机。洗衣房的旁边是餐厅和厨房，再过去才是客厅。小高站在门外，看着自己的新家，非常高兴。

Questions (True/False):

a. (　)　這個房子有五個房間。

　　　　这个房子有五个房间。

b. (　)　小高不用到外邊，可以在家洗衣服。

　　　　小高不用到外边，可以在家洗衣服。

c. (　)　要是小高的朋友來家裏聊天、吃飯，他們應該到樓
　　　　上去。

　　　　要是小高的朋友来家里聊天、吃饭，他们应该到楼
　　　　上去。

**E.** What does the sign say? _____

**F.**

這個商店賣不賣紙和筆？你怎麼知道？

这个商店卖不卖纸和笔？你怎么知道？

# IV. Writing and Grammar Exercises

## A. Building Characters

Form a character by combining the given components as instructed. Then write a word, a phrase, or a short sentence in which that character appears.

**1.** 左邊一個"毛"，右邊兩個"火"
左边一个"毛"，右边两个"火"，
是 _____ 的 _____。

**2.** 左邊一個"木"，右邊一個"東"
左边一个"木"，右边一个"东"，
是 _____ 的 _____。

**3.** 上邊一個"口"，下邊兩個"口"
上边一个"口"，下边两个"口"，
是 _____ 的 _____。

**4.** 左邊一個"火"，右邊一個"一共"的"共"
左边一个"火"，右边一个"一共"的"共"，
是 _____ 的 _____。

**B.** Answer the following questions based on your own situation. (INTERPERSONAL)

**1. A:** 學校附近的飯館，你比較喜歡哪一家？
學校附近的饭馆，你比较喜欢哪一家？

**B:** _____ 。

**2. A:** 你覺得住校內比較省錢，還是住校外比較省錢？
你觉得住校内比较省钱，还是住校外比较省钱？

**B:** _____ 。

**3. A:** 學校裏的哪一棟樓比較新？
学校里的哪一栋楼比较新？

**B:** _____ 。

**C.** Complete the following dialogues using 比較/比较.

> EXAMPLE:
>
> **A:** 這個店的傢具太貴了，我想看看別的店怎麼樣。
> 这个店的家具太贵了，我想看看别的店怎么样。
>
> **B:** <u>這個店的傢具雖然比較貴</u>，但是比別的店都好得多。
> <u>这个店的家具虽然比较贵</u>，但是比别的店都好得多。

**1. A:** 我不想住校，宿舍房間太小了。
　　　　我不想住校，宿舍房间太小了。

　　**B:** ＿＿＿＿＿＿＿＿＿＿＿＿，但是離教室近，上課很方便。
　　　　＿＿＿＿＿＿＿＿＿＿＿＿，但是离教室近，上课很方便。

**2. A:** 這台洗衣機和烘乾機太吵了，應該買新的。
　　　　这台洗衣机和烘干机太吵了，应该买新的。

　　**B:** ＿＿＿＿＿＿＿＿＿＿＿＿＿＿，但是還可以用。
　　　　＿＿＿＿＿＿＿＿＿＿＿＿＿＿，但是还可以用。

**3. A:** 你怎麼帶我來這家餐館？你看他們的桌子椅子那麼舊。
　　　　你怎么带我来这家餐馆？你看他们的桌子椅子那么旧。

　　**B:** ＿＿＿＿＿＿＿＿＿＿＿＿，但是菜又好吃又便宜。
　　　　＿＿＿＿＿＿＿＿＿＿＿＿，但是菜又好吃又便宜。

**D.** Rewrite the following sentences using 得很.

> EXAMPLE:
>
> 那家飯館的菜非常地道。→ <u>那家飯館的菜地道得很</u>。
> 那家饭馆的菜非常地道。→ <u>那家饭馆的菜地道得很</u>。

**1.** 他住的那棟宿舍非常安靜。
　　他住的那栋宿舍非常安静。→ ＿＿＿＿＿＿＿＿＿＿＿。

**2.** 這個學校非常安全。
　　这个学校非常安全。→ ＿＿＿＿＿＿＿＿＿＿＿。

**3.** 那家商店非常遠。
　　那家商店非常远。→ ＿＿＿＿＿＿＿＿＿＿＿。

**E.** Complete the following dialogues using 恐怕.

EXAMPLE:

**A:** 哎，你的房間怎麼這麼熱？

哎，你的房间怎么这么热？

**B:** 我也不知道，<u>恐怕是空調壞了</u>。

我也不知道，<u>恐怕是空调坏了</u>。

**1. A:** 他明天能來嗎？

他明天能来吗？

**B:** 他這兩天非常忙，_____。

他这两天非常忙，_____。

**2. A:** 我剛下課，肚子餓得很。我想去學生餐廳吃晚飯。

我刚下课，肚子饿得很。我想去学生餐厅吃晚饭。

**B:** 可是現在已經快九點了。這麼晚了，_____。

可是现在已经快九点了。这么晚了，_____。

**3. A:** 你覺得我應該買幾個書架？

你觉得我应该买几个书架？

**B:** 你的房間不大，如果書架太多，_____，
最好只買一個。

你的房间不大，如果书架太多，_____，
最好只买一个。

**F.** Rearrange the following words into complete sentences. Pay attention to the Chinese word order.

**1.** 書　　一本　　買了　　我妹妹　　很有意思的

书　　一本　　买了　　我妹妹　　很有意思的

→_____

**2.** 從北京　　前天　　我　　是　　來的　　坐飛機

从北京　　前天　　我　　是　　来的　　坐飞机

→_____

3. 六個月　　兩年前　　工作了　　他　　在中國

　 六个月　　两年前　　工作了　　他　　在中国

→＿＿＿＿＿＿＿＿＿＿＿＿＿＿＿＿＿＿＿＿＿＿＿＿＿＿

4. 一些　在那家飯館　我們　昨天　很地道的　吃了　中國菜

　 一些　在那家饭馆　我们　昨天　很地道的　吃了　中国菜

→＿＿＿＿＿＿＿＿＿＿＿＿＿＿＿＿＿＿＿＿＿＿＿＿＿＿

5. 寫　　中國字　　小王　　很快　　寫得

　 写　　中国字　　小王　　很快　　写得

→＿＿＿＿＿＿＿＿＿＿＿＿＿＿＿＿＿＿＿＿＿＿＿＿＿＿

**G.** Describe the following scenes. Don't forget to mention the background, and if applicable, what the person is wearing. Remember to use 著/着 in your description. (PRESENTATIONAL)

1.

＿＿＿＿＿＿＿＿＿＿＿＿＿＿＿＿＿＿＿＿＿＿＿＿＿＿＿○

2.

＿＿＿＿＿＿＿＿＿＿＿＿＿＿＿＿＿＿＿＿＿＿＿＿＿＿＿○

3.

＿＿＿＿＿＿＿＿＿＿＿＿＿＿＿＿＿＿＿＿＿＿＿＿＿＿＿○

**H.** Translate the following exchanges into Chinese. (PRESENTATIONAL)

**1. A:** Where is your roommate from?

**B:** He's from New York.

_____

_____

**2. A:** I am starving.

**B:** Then let's go eat.

_____

_____

**3. A:** Does the store on campus sell furniture?

**B:** No, the campus stores generally don't sell furniture. They only sell daily necessities and stationery.

_____

_____

**I.** Translate the following sentences into Chinese. Pay attention to the Chinese word order, especially the position of time and place words. (PRESENTATIONAL)

**1.** I read a new book in the library yesterday afternoon.

_____

_____

**2.** My brother drove from Northern California to Southern California last weekend to visit a friend.

_____

_____

**3.** He was doing laundry on the second floor when his father called.

_____

_____

**4.** Little Zhang is going to play basketball with his friends after class.

_____

_____

**J.** Translate the following sentences into Chinese. Note that the modifier/attributive always precedes the modified/head of the noun. (PRESENTATIONAL)

**1.** This is the restaurant that my roommate mentioned.

_____

**2.** The dorm where I used to live was very small and very old.

_____

**3.** The food that your mom made last night was extremely tasty.

_____

**4.** The bookstore we went to this morning also sells sportswear.

_____

**K.** Translate the following passages into Chinese using the grammar points and vocabulary items from this lesson. (PRESENTATIONAL)

**1.** Near the campus there is a Chinese restaurant and a Japanese restaurant. The Japanese restaurant is rather expensive. The Chinese restaurant is much cheaper than the Japanese restaurant. Both restaurants are very close to the campus. It's really convenient.

_____

_____

_____

_____

**2.** This is Little Zhang's room. There is a bed in the middle of the room. On the bed there is a blanket and a comforter. On the right side of the room is a wardrobe. However, the wardrobe is empty. There's a bookshelf on the left side of the room. There are some books on the shelf.

_____

_____

_____

_____

**3.** I am moving into the dorm in a few days. The dorm is relatively new. My room is close to the bathroom. There are washers and dryers on my floor. It's really convenient to live there. However, I'm afraid it will be a bit noisy.

_____

_____

_____

_____

**L.** Describe your living quarters. Be sure to mention the location, the layout of your room, whether it is quiet for study and convenient for shopping, and finally whether you like living there and why. (PRESENTATIONAL)

## M. Storytelling (PRESENTATIONAL)

Write a story in Chinese based on the four cartoons below. Make sure that your story has a beginning, a middle, and an end. Also make sure that the transition from one picture to the next is smooth and logical.

1

2

3

4

# I. Listening Comprehension

## A. Textbook Content (INTERPRETIVE)

Listen to the recording for the Textbook and answer the questions in English.

**1.** Why did Zhang Tianming want to go to a Chinese restaurant?

_____

**2.** Who went to the restaurant with Zhang Tianming?

_____

**3.** Which people are more familiar with the menu of the restaurant?

_____

**4.** What did they order?

_____

**5.** When Ke Lin and Lin Xuemei eat at a Chinese restaurant, do they always order the same types of dishes? Why or why not?

_____

## B. Workbook Dialogue (INTERPRETIVE)

Listen to the recording for the Workbook and answer the questions.

Questions (True/False):

( )  **1.** The restaurant has been in business for almost a decade.

( )  **2.** The Zhang family moved from Guangdong to Shanghai many years ago.

( )  **3.** The dishes in the restaurant are typically spicy and salty.

( )  **4.** The male speaker has never dined in the restaurant.

Questions (Multiple Choice):

( )  **5.** Which of the following best describes the man's perception of Chinese cuisine?

    **a.** All Chinese restaurants use heavy ingredients and spices.

    **b.** The major Chinese cooking styles are clear-cut and mutually exclusive categories.

    **c.** The only authentic Chinese cuisine is Sichuan style.

( )  **6.** Which of the following best describes the woman's attitude toward Chinese restaurants?

    **a.** A good Chinese restaurant must be either Shanghai or Guangdong style.

    **b.** A good Chinese restaurant must serve good beef with Chinese broccoli.

    **c.** A good Chinese restaurant doesn't have to belong to a major cooking style.

## C. Workbook Narratives

**1.** Listen to the recording for the Workbook and list in English at least three reasons why Little Chen quit his job. (INTERPRETIVE)

    **a.** _____

    **b.** _____

    **c.** _____

**2.** Listen to the passage and answer in English:

In what three ways do the Chinese and Americans differ when it comes to dining out? (INTERPRETIVE)

    **a.** _____

    **b.** _____

    **c.** _____

**3.** Listen to the passage and answer the question from the recording in Chinese. (INTERPRETIVE AND PRESENTATIONAL)

| | |
|---|---|
| 涼拌黄瓜 | 凉拌黄瓜 |
| 家常豆腐 | 家常豆腐 |
| 清蒸魚 | 清蒸鱼 |
| 糖醋魚 | 糖醋鱼 |
| 紅燒雞 | 红烧鸡 |
| 芥蘭牛肉 | 芥兰牛肉 |
| 酸辣湯 | 酸辣汤 |
| 小白菜湯 | 小白菜汤 |
| 菠菜豆腐湯 | 菠菜豆腐汤 |
| 米飯 | 米饭 |
| 可樂 | 可乐 |
| 冰茶 | 冰茶 |
| 冰咖啡 | 冰咖啡 |
| 熱茶 | 热茶 |
| 熱咖啡 | 热咖啡 |

_____

_____

_____

_____

_____

_____

## D. Workbook Listening Rejoinder (INTERPERSONAL)

In this section, you will hear two people talking. After hearing the first speaker, select the best from the four possible responses given by the second speaker.

_____

# II. Speaking Exercises

**A.** Practice asking and answering the following questions. (INTERPERSONAL)

**1.** 你吃過中國菜嗎？學校附近有沒有中國飯館兒？

你吃过中国菜吗？学校附近有没有中国饭馆儿？

**2.** 你吃素嗎？

你吃素吗？

**3.** 你先喝湯再吃菜，還是先吃菜再喝湯？還是一邊吃菜、
一邊喝湯？

你先喝汤再吃菜，还是先吃菜再喝汤？还是一边吃菜、
一边喝汤？

**B.** Practice speaking on the following topics. (INTERPERSONAL)

**1.** 你喜歡吃什麼口味的菜？鹹的？甜的？辣的？
還是清淡的？

你喜欢吃什么口味的菜？咸的？甜的？辣的？
还是清淡的？

**2.** 如果在中國飯館點菜，你會點什麼菜？

如果在中国饭馆点菜，你会点什么菜？

**C.** Have a dialogue with your partner about dining out. Invite him/her to eat at a Chinese restaurant. Decide on a place, date, and time. Ask about your partner's favorite restaurants and dishes. Discuss your dietary preferences or restrictions and decide which dishes to order based on both people's tastes.

# III. Reading Comprehension

## A. Building Words

Complete this section by writing the characters, the *pinyin*, and the English equivalent of each new word formed. Guess the meaning before you use a dictionary to confirm.

1. "名字" 的 "名" + "菜單" 的 "單"
   "名字" 的 "名" + "菜单" 的 "单"

   → _____ _____ _____
              new word    *pinyin*    English

2. "雞" + "蛋糕" 的 "蛋"
   "鸡" + "蛋糕" 的 "蛋"

   → _____ _____ _____

3. "清蒸魚" 的 "魚" + "烘乾" 的 "乾"
   "清蒸鱼" 的 "鱼" + "烘干" 的 "干"

   → _____ _____ _____

4. "汽車" 的 "汽" + "油"
   "汽车" 的 "汽" + "油"

   → _____ _____ _____

5. "出去" 的 "出" + "門口" 的 "口"
   "出去" 的 "出" + "门口" 的 "口"

   → _____ _____ _____

**B.** Draw a line connecting the cuisine with its signature flavor.

| | | |
|---|---|---|
| 四川菜 | 四川菜 | 清淡 |
| 廣東菜 | 广东菜 | 甜 |
| 上海菜 | 上海菜 | 辣 |

**C.** Take a look at these dishes. Which of them do you think are vegetarian? Use check marks to indicate your answers. (INTERPRETIVE)

| Traditional | Simplified | Yes | No | Sometimes |
|---|---|---|---|---|
| 涼拌黃瓜 | 凉拌黄瓜 | | | |
| 家常豆腐 | 家常豆腐 | | | |
| 紅燒牛肉 | 红烧牛肉 | | | |
| 芥蘭牛肉 | 芥兰牛肉 | | | |
| 清蒸魚 | 清蒸鱼 | | | |
| 糖醋魚 | 糖醋鱼 | | | |
| 酸辣湯 | 酸辣汤 | | | |
| 菠菜豆腐湯 | 菠菜豆腐汤 | | | |

**D.** Read the passage and answer in Chinese the question at the end. (INTERPRETIVE AND PRESENTATIONAL)

(TRADITIONAL)

　　有的人覺得應該想吃什麼就吃什麼，不要怕油多。有的人覺得菜越清淡越好，應該多吃青菜，少吃肉，特別是少吃牛肉。做菜的時候，要少放油，少放鹽。你覺得呢？

(SIMPLIFIED)

　　有的人觉得应该想吃什么就吃什么，不要怕油多。有的人觉得菜越清淡越好，应该多吃青菜，少吃肉，特别是少吃牛肉。做菜的时候，要少放油，少放盐。你觉得呢？

_____

_____

**E.** Read the passage and answer the questions in English. (INTERPRETIVE)

(TRADITIONAL)

小柯常到學校附近的一家中國飯館吃飯。那家飯館的菜又便宜又地道，他是那兒的常客，服務員都認識他。小柯今天又去那兒吃午飯。但是他一進門，就覺得跟以前不一樣了。這家飯館的菜以前非常清淡，可是今天怎麼那麼油？還有，今天的服務員他一個都不認識。菜單上的菜也比以前貴多了。除了這些以外，他點的菜裏還放了很多味精。他想下次再也不到這家飯館來吃飯了。

(SIMPLIFIED)

小柯常到学校附近的一家中国饭馆吃饭。那家饭馆的菜又便宜又地道，他是那儿的常客，服务员都认识他。小柯今天又去那儿吃午饭。但是他一进门，就觉得跟以前不一样了。这家饭馆的菜以前非常清淡，可是今天怎么那么油？还有，今天的服务员他一个都不认识。菜单上的菜也比以前贵多了。除了这些以外，他点的菜里还放了很多味精。他想下次再也不到这家饭馆来吃饭了。

Questions

**1.** What attracted Little Ke to the restaurant before?

_____

**2.** What four changes did Little Ke notice on this visit?

_____

**3.** Did he eat? How do you know?

_____

**4.** Will he eat there again?

_____

**F.** Read the passage and answer the following true/false questions. (INTERPRETIVE)

吃醋: to eat vinegar; to be jealous

(TRADITIONAL)

今天是太太的生日，李先生很早就從公司回家，想給太太做一個紅燒魚。魚做好了，李先生覺得味道太淡。他加了一點鹽，還是太淡，又加了一點鹽，還是太淡。李先生覺得不對，才知道自己把糖當成鹽了。他就在菜裏放了一些醋，把紅燒魚做成了糖醋魚。太太笑著說："我不是愛吃醋的女人。"李先生說："多吃醋對身體有好處！"

(SIMPLIFIED)

今天是太太的生日，李先生很早就从公司回家，想给太太做一个红烧鱼。鱼做好了，李先生觉得味道太淡。他加了一点盐，还是太淡，又加了一点盐，还是太淡。李先生觉得不对，才知道自己把糖当成盐了。他就在菜里放了一些醋，把红烧鱼做成了糖醋鱼。太太笑着说："我不是爱吃醋的女人。"李先生说："多吃醋对身体有好处！"

Questions (True/False):

( )  **1.** Mr. Li didn't go to work today.
( )  **2.** Mr. Li put a lot of salt in the fish.
( )  **3.** Vinegar is one of the essential ingredients in Mr. Li's fish recipe.
( )  **4.** Mr. Li put a lot of vinegar in the fish because Mrs. Li likes vinegar.
( )  **5.** Mrs. Li does not consider herself a jealous woman.

**G.** Read the passage and answer the question in English. (INTERPRETIVE)

(TRADITIONAL)

這是我從我的中文老師那兒聽來的：

今天是小明的生日，爸爸媽媽帶他到飯館吃飯。爸爸說他們要去的飯館是小朋友最喜歡的。但是到了飯館門前，小明看見飯館的名字，就哭著說："我不進去！"媽媽說："你為什麼不進去呀？"小明說："我怕！"

爸爸看到飯館的名字是"友朋小吃"，就笑了起來。你們知道小明為什麼怕，爸爸為什麼笑嗎？

(SIMPLIFIED)

这是我从我的中文老师那儿听来的：

今天是小明的生日，爸爸妈妈带他到饭馆吃饭。爸爸说他们要去的饭馆是小朋友最喜欢的。但是到了饭馆门前，小明看见饭馆的名字，就哭着说："我不进去！"妈妈说："你为什么不进去呀？"小明说："我怕！"

爸爸看到饭馆的名字是"友朋小吃"，就笑了起来。你们知道小明为什么怕，爸爸为什么笑吗？

___

Hint: the sign can be read as an anagram. Ask your teacher to explain how shop signs, placards, and newspaper headlines were traditionally inscribed in Chinese culture.

**H.** This is a set menu for a multi-course meal. Try your best to tell your friends who don't read Chinese what's on the menu. (INTERPRETIVE)

| | |
|---|---|
| ★ 前菜 | ★ 前菜 |
| ★ 沙拉 | ★ 沙拉 |
| ★ 湯 | ★ 汤 |
| ★ 主餐 | ★ 主餐 |
| ★ 甜點 | ★ 甜点 |
| ★ 飲料 | ★ 饮料 |

_____

_____

_____

_____

**I.** This is an excerpt from a cookbook. What's the dish? Is it vegetarian? (INTERPRETIVE)

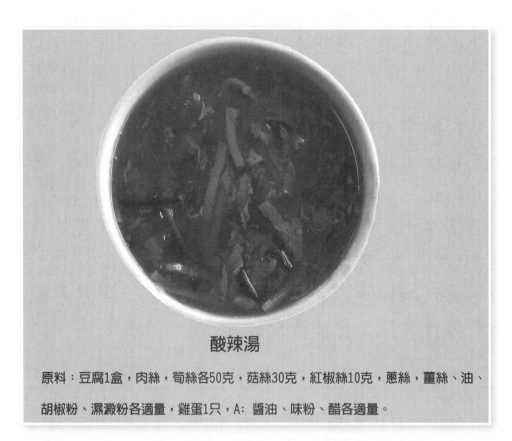

**酸辣湯**

原料：豆腐1盒，肉絲，筍絲各50克，菇絲30克，紅椒絲10克，蔥絲，薑絲、油、胡椒粉、濕澱粉各適量，雞蛋1只，A：醬油、味粉、醋各適量。

**酸辣汤**

原料：豆腐1盒，肉丝，笋丝各50克，菇丝30克，红椒丝10克，葱丝，姜丝、油、胡椒粉、湿淀粉各适量，鸡蛋1只，A：酱油、味粉、醋各适量。

# IV. Writing and Grammar Exercises

## A. Building Characters

Form a character by combining the given components as instructed. Then write a word, a phrase, or a short sentence in which that character appears.

**1.** 左邊一個 "魚"，右邊一個 "羊"
左边一个 "鱼"，右边一个 "羊"，
是 ＿＿＿＿＿＿＿ 的 ＿＿＿＿ 。

**2.** 左邊三點水，右邊兩個 "火"
左边三点水，右边两个 "火"，，
是 ＿＿＿＿＿＿＿ 的 ＿＿＿＿ 。

**3.** 左邊三點水，右邊一個 "自由" 的 "由"
左边三点水，右边一个 "自由" 的 "由"，
是 ＿＿＿＿＿＿＿ 的 ＿＿＿＿ 。

**4.** 左邊一個 "木"，右邊一個 "每天" 的 "每"
左边一个 "木"，右边一个 "每天" 的 "每"，
是 ＿＿＿＿＿＿＿ 的 ＿＿＿＿ 。

**B.** Answer the questions using the phrases in parentheses as topics in a topic-comment sentence.
(INTERPRETIVE AND PRESENTATIONAL)

EXAMPLE:

**A:** 學校附近有很多飯館，還有一家中國餐館，不知道那兒
的菜怎麼樣？ (那家餐館)
学校附近有很多饭馆，还有一家中国餐馆，不知道那儿
的菜怎么样？ (那家餐馆)

**B:** 那家餐館我去過。菜做得很地道
那家餐馆我去过。菜做得很地道

**1. A:** 張天明認識柯林的女朋友嗎？ (柯林的女朋友)
张天明认识柯林的女朋友吗？

**B:** ＿＿＿＿＿＿＿＿＿＿＿＿＿＿＿＿＿＿＿＿＿＿＿＿＿＿＿＿＿＿＿＿ 。

**2. A:** 張天明已經適應宿舍的生活了嗎？　　　　(宿舍的生活)

　　張天明已经适应宿舍的生活了吗？　　　　(宿舍的生活)

　　**B:** _____ 。

**3. A:** 你吃過四川菜嗎？味道怎麼樣？　　　　(四川菜)

　　你吃过四川菜吗？味道怎么样？　　　　(四川菜)

　　**B:** _____ 。

**2. A:** 你會寫第二課的生詞嗎？　　　　(第二課的生詞)

　　你会写第二课的生词吗？　　　　(第二课的生词)

　　**B:** _____ 。

**C.** Paraphrase the following sentences using 一···就···.

**1.** 這課的語法很容易，老師剛講完，我就懂了。

　　这课的语法很容易，老师刚讲完，我就懂了。

　　→ _____ 。

**2.** 他很聰明，什麼字，你教他，他很快就會了。

　　他很聪明，什么字，你教他，他很快就会了。

　　→ _____ 。

**3.** 那個地方很近，很快就走到了。

　　那个地方很近，很快就走到了。

　　→ _____ 。

**D.** Rewrite the following sentences using 又···又···.

EXAMPLE:

那棟宿舍很新，也很漂亮。→ 那棟宿舍又新又漂亮。

那栋宿舍很新，也很漂亮。→ 那栋宿舍又新又漂亮。

**1.** 我媽媽做的牛肉很嫩，而且很香。

　　我妈妈做的牛肉很嫩，而且很香。

　　→ _____ 。

**2.** 那家飯館的菜不但很油、而且很鹹。

那家饭馆的菜不但很油、而且很咸。

→ _____ 。

**3.** 聽說那家商店的青菜水果非常新鮮，而且很便宜。

听说那家商店的青菜水果非常新鲜，而且很便宜。

→ _____ 。

**E.** Based on your own situation or opinion, answer the following questions using 這就要看⋯了/这就要看⋯了.

**1. A:** 你下個學期還要學中文嗎？

你下个学期还要学中文吗？

**B:** _____ 。

**2. A:** 你這個週末打算做什麼？

你这个周末打算做什么？

**B:** _____ 。

**3. A:** 你覺得大學新生應該住校內還是住校外？

你觉得大学新生应该住校内还是住校外？

**B:** _____ 。

**F.** Based on the information given, describe what the characters in the textbook like or dislike most, using 特別是.

EXAMPLE:

→ 張天明喜歡吃肉，特別是雞。

張天明喜欢吃肉，特别是鸡。

1. →＿＿＿＿＿＿＿＿＿＿＿＿＿＿＿＿＿＿＿

2. →＿＿＿＿＿＿＿＿＿＿＿＿＿＿＿＿＿＿＿

3. →＿＿＿＿＿＿＿＿＿＿＿＿＿＿＿＿＿＿＿

**G.** Fill in the blanks with 的, 地, or 得.

(TRADITIONAL)

我問同學他們覺得附近哪一家餐館＿＿＿＿＿＿＿菜做＿＿＿＿＿＿＿最好吃。他們告訴我學校南邊那家中國飯館＿＿＿＿＿＿＿菜最好。聽說，那家餐館上菜上＿＿＿＿＿＿＿快，菜也做＿＿＿＿＿＿＿很地道。地方又大又安靜。大家都喜歡在那兒慢慢兒＿＿＿＿＿＿＿吃，邊吃飯，邊聊天。

(SIMPLIFIED)

我问同学他们觉得附近哪一家餐馆＿＿＿＿＿＿＿菜做＿＿＿＿＿＿＿最好吃。他们告诉我学校南边那家中国饭馆＿＿＿＿＿＿＿菜最好。听说，那家餐馆上菜上＿＿＿＿＿＿＿快，菜也做＿＿＿＿＿＿＿很地道。地方又大又安静。大家都喜欢在那儿慢慢儿＿＿＿＿＿＿＿吃，边吃饭，边聊天。

**H.** Fill in the blanks with the words and phrases provided. (PRESENTATIONAL)

(TRADITIONAL)

| 要不然　　又…又…　　這就要看　　非常　　比較　　特別是 |
| --- |

我覺得這家餐館的菜做得＿＿＿＿＿＿＿好，＿＿＿＿＿＿他
們的清蒸魚，＿＿＿＿＿＿新鮮＿＿＿＿＿＿好吃。但是
有的人覺得他們的菜太清淡。所以如果你要問這家餐館的菜好
不好，＿＿＿＿＿＿你的口味了。我自己吃的＿＿＿＿＿＿
清淡，＿＿＿＿＿＿，就不會說這家餐館的菜好吃了。

(SIMPLIFIED)

| 要不然　　又…又…　　这就要看　　非常　　比较　　特别是 |
| --- |

我觉得这家餐馆的菜做得＿＿＿＿＿＿＿好，＿＿＿＿＿＿他
们的清蒸鱼，＿＿＿＿＿＿新鲜＿＿＿＿＿＿好吃。但是
有的人觉得他们的菜太清淡。所以如果你要问这家餐馆的菜好
不好，＿＿＿＿＿＿你的口味了。我自己吃的＿＿＿＿＿＿
清淡，＿＿＿＿＿＿，就不会说这家餐馆的菜好吃了。

**I.** Translate the following sentences into Chinese. (PRESENTATIONAL)

**1.** I finished reading the book I bought yesterday. (topic-comment)

＿＿＿＿＿＿＿＿＿＿＿＿＿＿＿＿＿＿＿＿＿＿＿＿＿＿＿

**2.** Your younger sister is very pretty. (長得/长得)

＿＿＿＿＿＿＿＿＿＿＿＿＿＿＿＿＿＿＿＿＿＿＿＿＿＿＿

**3.** The steamed fish tastes excellent.

＿＿＿＿＿＿＿＿＿＿＿＿＿＿＿＿＿＿＿＿＿＿＿＿＿＿＿

**4.** The beef and broccoli at this restaurant is superb. The beef is tender and smells wonderful. ( 又 ⋯ 又 ⋯ )

_____

**5.** Could I trouble you not to put any MSG in the food?

_____

**J.** Translate the following passages into Chinese. (PRESENTATIONAL)

**1.** Ke Lin and Zhang Tianming went out to eat last night. Ke Lin drove very fast and they got to Chinatown very quickly. The dishes that they ordered were all delicious. As soon as they finished eating, they went back to school. While driving, they talked and laughed. They were very happy.

_____

_____

_____

_____

**2.** I hadn't had Chinese food for three weeks and was thinking about having some authentic Chinese food in Chinatown. As it happened, my friend Little Lin also wanted to have some Chinese food. But neither of us had a car. It took us an hour to walk there. We ordered three dishes, and they smelled good and tasted great. We both felt that we should have ordered more.

_____

_____

_____

_____

**K.** Write a restaurant review. In your review, comment on the décor of the restaurant, the service, the prices, and your favorite dishes. (PRESENTATIONAL)

## L. Storytelling (PRESENTATIONAL)

Write a story in Chinese based on the four cartoons below. Make sure that your story has a beginning, a middle, and an end. Also make sure that the transition from one picture to the next is smooth and logical.

**1**

**2**

**3**

**4**

第四課　　買東西
第四课　　买东西

# I. Listening Comprehension

## A. Textbook Content (INTERPRETIVE)

Listen to the recording for the Textbook and answer the questions in English.

**1.** Why doesn't Zhang Tianming like the clothes that his mother bought for him?

_____

**2.** What is Zhang Tianming's philosophy of shopping for clothes?

_____

**3.** What are Ke Lin's criteria for buying clothes?

_____

**4.** With whom does Lisa agree?

_____

## B. Workbook Dialogue (INTERPRETIVE)

Listen to the recording for the Workbook and answer the questions.

Questions (True/False):

( )　**1.** The woman urges the man not to worry about her wardrobe.

( )　**2.** The man and woman went shopping together last weekend.

( )　**3.** The woman has not bought much clothing recently because she wants to save money.

( )　**4.** The woman thinks her clothes are not only all name-brand, but also fashionable.

( )　**5.** It is difficult for the woman to buy clothes because she is too picky about prices.

## C. Workbook Narratives

1. Listen to the recording for the Workbook and answer the questions in English. (INTERPRETIVE)

   **a.** In the past, how did the Chinese pay for their purchases?

   _____

   **b.** What has changed about Chinese shoppers' methods of payment?

   _____

   **c.** In what way is shopping in China different from shopping in most states in the United States?

   _____

2. Listen to the passage and answer the following questions in English. (INTERPRETIVE)

   **a.** What does Little Lin look for when buying clothes?

   _____

   **b.** What does Little Wang think about Little Lin's criteria for choosing what to wear?

   _____

   **c.** Would you prefer to go shopping with Lin or Wang? Why?

   _____

3. Listen to the passage and answer the following questions in English. (INTERPRETIVE)

   **a.** What is the name of the shopping center?

   _____

   **b.** How many floors are there?

   _____

   **c.** If you want to buy shoes, which floor should you go to?

   _____

   **d.** Why is there a sale at the shopping center? How big is the discount?

   _____

   **e.** In addition to the sale, what is the extra incentive for customers?

   _____

4. Listen to the passage and answer the following questions in English. (INTERPRETIVE)

   **a.** What does the hotel provide for its guests?

   _____

   **b.** How can the guests pay their bills?

   _____

**c.** Which amenity would you like the most?

_____

**d.** What is the disadvantage of staying at this hotel?

_____

**e.** If the room rate is $100 per night, how much does it cost to stay at the hotel for one night including tax?

_____

### D. Workbook Listening Rejoinder (INTERPERSONAL)

In this section, you will hear two people talking. After hearing the first speaker, select the best from the four possible responses given by the second speaker.

_____

# II. Speaking Exercises

**A.** Practice asking and answering the following questions. (INTERPERSONAL)

1. 你一般多久買一次衣服？
   你一般多久买一次衣服？

2. 你現在身上穿的衣服/襯衫/褲子是什麼顏色的？
   你现在身上穿的衣服/衬衫/裤子是什么颜色的？

3. 你買衣服的標準是什麼？
   你买衣服的标准是什么？

4. 一般來说，買東西的時候，你付現金還是用信用卡？
   一般来说，买东西的时候，你付现金还是用信用卡？

5. 你現在住的州買衣服需要付税嗎？
   你现在住的州买衣服需要付税吗？

**B.** Practice speaking on the following topics.

1. 你跟你的朋友一起去買東西，他看到什麼都想買，你怎麼讓他少買一些？
   你跟你的朋友一起去买东西，他看到什么都想买，你怎么让他少买一些？

2.請你説説你對名牌衣服的看法。你買衣服一定要買名牌的
嗎？為什麼？

請你说说你对名牌衣服的看法。你买衣服一定要买名牌的
吗？为什么？ (PRESENTATIONAL)

3. You are a salesperson and have to sell this T-shirt. Talk to a potential customer about
the T-shirt based on the information on the clothing label and tag, and try to convince
the customer that the T-shirt is wonderful in style, color, material, and price and is
ideal for him or her. (PRESENTATIONAL)

Name Brand

Original: $40

Now: $20

Made in China

100% Cotton

Machine Wash

Tumble Dry

# III. Reading Comprehension

## A. Building Words

Complete this section by writing the characters, the *pinyin*, and the English equivalent of each new
word formed. Guess the meaning before you use a dictionary to confirm.

1. "長短"的"短" + "牛仔褲"的"褲"
   "长短"的"短" + "牛仔裤"的"裤"

   → _____ _____ _____
          new word    *pinyin*    English

2. "校内"的"内" + "衣服"的"衣"

    → _____ _____ _____

3. "汽車"的"車"＋"牌子"的"牌"
   "汽车"的"车"＋"牌子"的"牌"

   → ＿＿＿＿＿  ＿＿＿＿＿  ＿＿＿＿＿

4. "吃藥"的"藥"＋"牙膏"的"膏"
   "吃药"的"药"＋"牙膏"的"膏"

   → ＿＿＿＿＿  ＿＿＿＿＿  ＿＿＿＿＿

5. "牙膏"的"牙"＋"刷卡"的"刷"

   → ＿＿＿＿＿  ＿＿＿＿＿  ＿＿＿＿＿

**B.** Read the passage and answer the following true/false questions. (INTERPRETIVE)

(TRADITIONAL)

　　柯林買衣服只要樣子、顏色、大小、長短合適就行，不在乎是不是名牌。他的女朋友林雪梅覺得名牌的衣服質量好得多，穿起來也更舒服。上個週末柯林買了一件襯衫，是雪梅最不喜歡的黃色，然後穿著去見她。雪梅一看見就叫起來："你怎麼買了一件這麼難看的衣服？"柯林笑著說："這是名牌的！難道你不喜歡？"

(SIMPLIFIED)

　　柯林买衣服只要样子、颜色、大小、长短合适就行，不在乎是不是名牌。他的女朋友林雪梅觉得名牌的衣服质量好得多，穿起来也更舒服。上个周末柯林买了一件衬衫，是雪梅最不喜欢的黄色，然后穿着去见她。雪梅一看见就叫起来："你怎么买了一件这么难看的衣服？"柯林笑着说："这是名牌的！难道你不喜欢？"

Questions (True/False)

( )  **1.**  Ke Lin has no standards when shopping for clothes.

( )  **2.**  To Lin Xuemei, a good brand means good quality.

( )  **3.**  Last weekend Ke Lin and Lin Xuemei went shopping together.

( )  **4.**  Ke Lin tried to make the point that brand-name clothes are not necessarily good.

**C.** Read the passage and check the boxes in the table based on the information given. Then answer in Chinese the question at the end of the passage. (INTERPRETIVE AND PRESENTATIONAL)

(TRADITIONAL)

　　小張買東西的標準是：只要是名牌的，無論樣子好不好，價錢貴不貴，他都要買。小林買東西跟小張不一樣，很在乎質量，而且要價錢便宜。他們兩個一起出去買衣服的時候，小張覺得小林只想省錢，不在乎牌子；小林覺得小張只想穿名牌兒，不在乎衣服樣子合適不合適。所以他們常常出去的時候很高興，回來的時候很不高興。

　　你呢？你會跟小張還是小林一起去買東西？為什麼？

(SIMPLIFIED)

　　小张买东西的标准是：只要是名牌的，无论样子好不好，价钱贵不贵，他都要买。小林买东西跟小张不一样，很在乎质量，而且要价钱便宜。他们两个一起出去买衣服的时候，小张觉得小林只想省钱，不在乎牌子；小林觉得小张只想穿名牌儿，不在乎衣服样子合适不合适。所以他们常常出去的时候很高兴，回来的时候很不高兴。

　　你呢？你会跟小张还是小林一起去买东西？为什么？

| | Brand name | Price | Style | Quality |
|---|---|---|---|---|
| Little Zhang | | | | |
| Little Lin | | | | |
| You | | | | |

Your answer: _____

_____

**D.** What does this sign say? (INTERPRETIVE)

**E.** Read the advertisement for a department store's sale and answer the questions. (INTERPRETIVE)

**1.** Which department will offer a forty percent discount?

**2.** Will every item in that department be forty percent off? How do you know?

**3.** Will customers get a discount if they go shopping on a Friday?

**F.** Since the mid-nineties, retailers from overseas have been setting up shop in coastal cities in mainland China. Upscale boutiques and department stores are now becoming quite commonplace in big cities. The following advertisement appeared in a Shanghai evening paper. Skim through it and complete the following tasks. (INTERPRETIVE)

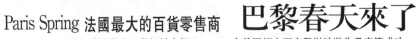

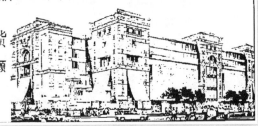

1. Circle the Chinese name of this store.

2. Circle the address of the store.

3. Circle the description that is used to convince the Chinese customer of the prestige of the store.

## IV. Writing and Grammar Exercises

### A. Building Characters

Form a character by combining the given components as indicated. Then write a word, a phrase, or a short sentence in which that character appears.

1. 左邊一個人字旁，右邊一個"子"
   左边一个人字旁，右边一个"子"，
   是 _____ 的 _____。

2. 上邊一個"雨"，下邊一個"而且"的"而"
   上边一个"雨"，下边一个"而且"的"而"，
   是 _____ 的 _____。

**3.** 上邊一個"高"，下邊一個"月"
上边一个"高"，下边一个"月"，
是 _____的 _____。

**4.** 左邊一個"米"，右邊一個"分鐘"的"分"
左边一个"米"，右边一个"分钟"的"分"，
是 _____的 _____。

**B.** Answer the following questions in Chinese. (INTERPERSONAL)

**1. A:** 今天是幾月幾號，星期幾？
今天是几月几号，星期几？

**B:** _____ 。

**2. A:** 這個學期開學多久了？
这个学期开学多久了？

**B:** _____ 。

**3. A:** 你一個星期上幾次中文課？什麼時候上？
你一个星期上几次中文课？什么时候上？

**B:** _____ 。

**4. A:** 你昨天做功課做了多長時間？
你昨天做功课做了多长时间？

**B:** _____ 。

**5. A:** 你多長時間沒聽錄音了？
你多长时间没听录音了？

**B:** _____ 。

**6. A:** 你多久洗一次衣服？
你多久洗一次衣服？

**B:** _____ 。

**7. A:** 從你住的地方開車到購物中心要開多長時間？
从你住的地方开车到购物中心要开多长时间？

**B:** _____ 。

**C.** Complete the following sentences using 什麼的／什么的.

EXAMPLE:

這個購物中心真大，<u>衣服、日用品什麼的</u>，你都能
買到。

这个购物中心真大，<u>衣服、日用品什么的</u>，你都能
买到。

**1.** 這家中國飯館的菜很好，＿＿＿＿＿＿＿＿＿＿＿＿＿，
都很地道。

这家中国饭馆的菜很好，＿＿＿＿＿＿＿＿＿＿＿＿＿，
都很地道。

**2.** 他買衣服很花時間，＿＿＿＿＿＿＿＿＿＿＿＿＿，他都
得看很久。

他买衣服很花时间，＿＿＿＿＿＿＿＿＿＿＿＿＿，他都
得看很久。

**3.** 跟他一起租房子真不容易，＿＿＿＿＿＿＿＿＿＿＿，
他都要問清楚。

跟他一起租房子真不容易，＿＿＿＿＿＿＿＿＿＿＿，
他都要问清楚。

**D.** Rewrite the following sentences using 無論…都／无论…都.

EXAMPLE:

這兩天他不太舒服，清蒸魚、芥蘭牛肉、菠菜豆腐什麼
的，他都不想吃。

这两天他不太舒服，清蒸鱼、芥兰牛肉、菠菜豆腐什么
的，他都不想吃。

→ <u>這兩天他不太舒服，無論什麼菜，他都不想吃。</u>
<u>这两天他不太舒服，无论什么菜，他都不想吃。</u>

1. 那個宿舍，早上吵，中午吵，下午吵，晚上也吵。
   那个宿舍，早上吵，中午吵，下午吵，晚上也吵。

   → _____ 。

2. 這個城市的稅很重。買吃的要稅，買穿的要付稅，買用
   的也要付稅。
   这个城市的税很重。买吃的要税，买穿的要付税，买用
   的也要付税。

   → _____ 。

3. 附近新開的購物中心非常大。吃的、穿的、用的、玩兒
   的，都能買到。
   附近新开的购物中心非常大。吃的、穿的、用的、玩儿
   的，都能买到。

   → _____ 。

人民幣一百元
人民币一百元

人民幣五十元
人民币五十元

**E.** Complete the following sentences using 要不然.

EXAMPLE:

租房子最好租帶家具的，<u>要不然得花很多錢買家具</u>。
租房子最好租帶家具的，<u>要不然得花很多钱买家具</u>。

1. 學中文最好天天聽錄音，_____ 。
   学中文最好天天听录音，_____ 。

**2.** 在中國飯館點菜，如果你不能吃比較油比較鹹的菜，就得
告訴服務員少放點兒鹽和油，_____。
在中国饭馆点菜，如果你不能吃比较油比较咸的菜，就得
告诉服务员少放点儿盐和油，_____。

**3.** 租房子最好不要租在大馬路旁邊的，_____。
租房子最好不要租在大马路旁边的，_____。

**F.** You disagree with your friend on many issues, but you are always tactful. You always acknowledge the partial validity of your friend's view before stating your own opinion.

Complete the following sentences using "Adj/V+是+Adj/V, 可是…."

EXAMPLE:

**A:** 你為什麼不喜歡去那家餐館吃飯？他們的菜做得很
地道。
你为什么不喜欢去那家餐馆吃饭？他们的菜做得很
地道。

**B:** 他們的菜地道是地道，可是有點油。
他们的菜地道是地道，可是有点油。

**1. A:** 中文太難了。
中文太难了。

**B:** _____，_____。

**2. A:** 住在校內很好，你為什麼要搬出去？
住在校内很好，你为什么要搬出去？

**B:** _____，_____。

**3. A:** 這棟樓那麼舊，你為什麼不搬到別的地方去？
这栋楼那么旧，你为什么不搬到别的地方去？

**B:** _____，_____。

**4. A:** 這條褲子你穿著很好看，為什麼不買？
这条裤子你穿着很好看，为什么不买？

**B:** _____，_____。

**G.** Complete the following sentences using 非…不可….

EXAMPLE:

天氣又熱又不舒服，<u>非下雨不可</u>，你別去打球了。
天气又热又不舒服，<u>非下雨不可</u>，你别去打球了。

1. 今天我母親過生日，晚上的生日晚會我_____。
　今天我母亲过生日，晚上的生日晚会我_____。

2. 他每次出去吃飯，_____，別的菜
　他都不喜歡吃。
　他每次出去吃饭，_____，别的菜
　他都不喜欢吃。

3. 你天天吃那麼多肉，又那麼喜歡吃糖，_____。
　你天天吃那么多肉，又那么喜欢吃糖，_____。

**H.** Translate the following passage into English. (PRESENTATIONAL)

(TRADITIONAL)

　小李只有在打折的時候才買衣服，一聽說哪家商店打折，就非去買不可。我説："打折的東西便宜是便宜，但是質量也差一些。"小李説："衣服便宜可以多買幾件，質量差一點没關係，穿壞了可以再買新的呀。"

(SIMPLIFIED)

　小李只有在打折的时候才买衣服，一听说哪家商店打折，就非去买不可。我说："打折的东西便宜是便宜，但是质量也差一些。"小李说："衣服便宜可以多买几件，质量差一点没关系，穿坏了可以再买新的呀。"

_____
_____
_____
_____

**I.** Translate the following sentences into Chinese. (PRESENTATIONAL)

**1.** Zhang Tianming doesn't have a car. He has to take the bus wherever he wants to go. (無論／无论…都…)

_____

**2.** They had dinner at a restaurant in Chinatown. The dishes that they ordered, such as Chinese broccoli, steamed fish, etc., were all very delicious. (什麼的／什么的)

_____

_____

**3. A:** I feel living on campus is better. It's very convenient.

_____

**B:** Living on campus is convenient, but it's too expensive. (Adj 是 Adj, 可是…)

_____

**4. A:** No matter what I buy, I always buy the cheapest (one).

_____

**B:** Are you telling me that you only care about the price and not the quality? (難道／难道)

_____

**5.** I won't buy this pair of shoes for my son. He will wear nothing but brand-name shoes. (非…不可…)

_____

**6.** Zhang Tianming wanted to buy a sweatsuit, but he left his credit card in his dorm. Therefore, he told the salesperson he would buy the sweatsuit next week. (於是／于是)

_____

_____

**J.** Translate the following sentences into Chinese. Pay special attention to the position of the time phrases. (PRESENTATIONAL)

**1. A:** How long has your teacher been teaching Chinese?

_____

**B:** My teacher has been teaching Chinese for five years.

_____

**2. A:** How long haven't you had any Chinese food?

_____

**B:** I haven't had any Chinese food for two weeks.

_____

**3. A:** How often do you do your laundry?

_____

**B:** I do my laundry once a week.

_____

**4. A:** How many hours did your roommate sleep last night?

_____

**B:** My roommate slept for three hours last night.

_____

**5. A:** How long do you work at the university bookstore every day?

_____

**B:** I work two hours at the university bookstore every day.

_____

**6.** The doctor said that you have to drink water ten times a day.

_____

**7.** Little Zhang e-mails his parents every two or three days.

_____

**8.**    He moved three times last year.

_____

**9.**    My brother hasn't bought any jeans for two years.

_____

**10.**    He lived in the dorm for six months and moved off campus last week.

_____

**K.** Translate the following conversation into Chinese. (PRESENTATIONAL)

**A:** Is this set of clothes pure cotton?

_____

**B:** Yes.

_____

**A:** If it's not pure cotton, I'll be allergic to it.

_____

**B:** Both the color and quality of the clothes are very good. (無論···還是···/
无论···还是···)

_____

**A:** I didn't bring cash. Can I use my credit card?

_____

**B:** I'm sorry. You can't use your card here. Why don't you come again tomorrow? I'm
really sorry.

_____

**L.** Translate the following passage into Chinese. (PRESENTATIONAL)

Little Zhang came to the United States from China in March last year. He has been living in New York State for more than a year, and hasn't had any authentic Chinese food for six months. Before he came to the United States, he heard that it was very convenient to live in the United States. But now that he is in America, he doesn't think so. Since he doesn't have a car, he has to ask friends for help wherever he goes. He misses his parents very much and plans to return to China right after he finishes his exams in December.

_____

_____

_____

_____

_____

_____

**M.** Write a brief essay on the following topic:

What I look for when shopping for clothes: preferences and criteria. (PRESENTATIONAL)

## N. Storytelling (PRESENTATIONAL)

Write a story in Chinese based on the four cartoons below. Make sure that your story has a beginning, a middle, and an end. Also make sure that the transition from one picture to the next is smooth and logical.

**1**

**2**

**3**

**4**

# I. Listening Comprehension

## A. Textbook Content (INTERPRETIVE)

Listen to the recording for the Textbook and answer the questions in English.

**1.** What courses is Zhang Tianming taking this semester?

_____

**2.** What do Zhang Tianming's parents want him to major in?

_____

**3.** What does Li Zhe plan to do after he graduates from college?

_____

**4.** What does Zhang Tianming think Li Zhe should do in order to become more competitive on the job market?

_____

## B. Workbook Dialogue (INTERPRETIVE)

Listen to the recording for the Workbook and answer the questions.

Questions (True/False):

( )  **1.**  The speakers are most likely mother and son.

( )  **2.**  Regarding his post-graduation plan, the man is not likely to follow his father's advice.

( )  **3.**  None of the courses the man is taking next semester will fulfill his major requirements.

( )  **4.**  The man is quite confident about his academic work next semester.

Questions (Multiple Choice):

( )  **5.** The woman suggests that the man take another course in computer science because she thinks that _____.

   **a.** it is required for his major

   **b.** it is easier than a course in finance

   **c.** it is more relevant to his future studies as a graduate student

( )  **6.** Which of the following is the university's requirement?

   **a.** All students must take at least one course in philosophy.

   **b.** All engineering students must take a course in philosophy.

   **c.** All graduating seniors must take a course in philosophy.

## C. Workbook Narratives

1.  Listen to the recording for the Workbook and answer the questions in English. (INTERPRETIVE)

   **a.** How many schools does the university have?

   _____

   **b.** What are they?

   _____

   **c.** Which school requires the highest tuition fees?

   _____

   **d.** Which school has the most students?

   _____

   **e.** Which school has the largest library?

   _____

   **f.** Which school has the best faculty?

   _____

   **g.** What is the controversy about?

   _____

   **h.** What are the two opposing positions?

   _____

2.  Listen to the recording for the Workbook and answer the questions in English. (INTERPRETIVE)

   **a.** Why are more and more students interested in having double majors?

   _____

   **b.** What two examples of double majors are mentioned in the passage?

   _____

**3.** Listen to the recording for the Workbook and answer the questions. (INTERPRETIVE)

    **a.** Little Lin's original plan: _____

    _____

    **b.** Little Lin's parents' suggestion: _____

    _____

    **c.** Little Lin's professor's advice: _____

    _____

    **d.** Your opinion in Chinese: _____

    _____

## D. Workbook Listening Rejoinder (INTERPERSONAL)

In this section, you will hear two people talking. After hearing the first speaker, select the best from the four possible responses given by the second speaker.

_____

# II. Speaking Exercises

**A.** Practice asking and answering the following questions. (INTERPERSONAL)

    **1.** 你這學期選了幾門課？
        你这学期选了几门课？

    **2.** 你最喜歡哪一門課？為什麼？
        你最喜欢哪一门课？为什么？

    **3.** 哪門課最讓你受不了？為什麼？
        哪门课最让你受不了？为什么？

    **4.** 你下個學期打算學幾個學分？什麼時候可以畢業？
        你下个学期打算学几个学分？什么时候可以毕业？

**B.** Practice speaking on the following topics. (PRESENTATIONAL)

    **1.** 請談談你這個學期的學習。
        请谈谈你这个学期的学习。

    **2.** 請談談你找誰討論選專業的事。為什麼？
        请谈谈你找谁讨论选专业的事。为什么？

3. 請談談你的專業以及畢業以後的打算。

請談談你的专业以及毕业以后的打算。

# III. Reading Comprehension

## A. Building Words

Complete this section by writing the characters, the *pinyin*, and the English equivalent of each new word formed. Guess the meaning before you use a dictionary to confirm.

1. "中國"的"國" + "世界"的"界"

"中国"的"国" + "世界"的"界"

→ _____ _____ _____

new word    *pinyin*    English

2. "指導"的"導" + "老師"的"師"

"指导"的"导" + "老师"的"师"

→ _____ _____ _____

3. "輕鬆"的"輕" + "方便"的"便"

"轻松"的"轻" + "方便"的"便"

→ _____ _____ _____

4. "數字"的"數" + "化學"的"學"

"数字"的"数" + "化学"的"学"

→ _____ _____ _____

5. "決定"的"決" + "比賽"的"賽"

"决定"的"决" + "比赛"的"赛"

→ _____ _____ _____

**B.** Answer the questions in English after reading the following passage. (INTERPRETIVE)

(TRADITIONAL)

小李是大學三年級的學生，因為他打算明年五月就畢業，所以每個學期都選六門課，每個暑假都實習。要是學分夠，他還打算拿雙學位。他的指導教授覺得他課選得太多了，建議他少選一點，要不然太累了，對身體健康沒有好處。小李說他希望早一點畢業，這樣他可以把大學第四年的錢省下來。至於累不累，他不在乎。

(SIMPLIFIED)

　　小李是大学三年级的学生，因为他打算明年五月就毕业，所以每个学期都选六门课，每个暑假都实习。要是学分够，他还打算拿双学位。他的指导教授觉得他课选得太多了，建议他少选一点，要不然太累了，对身体健康没有好处。小李说他希望早一点毕业，这样他可以把大学第四年的钱省下来。至于累不累，他不在乎。

Questions:

**1.** Why does Little Li want to graduate one year early?

_____

**2.** What did Little Li's advisor say to him?

_____

**3.** Do you think it is possible for Little Li to achieve his goal? Why or why not?

_____

**4.** Would you do the same thing if you were Little Li? Why or why not?

_____

**C.** Read the passage and answer the questions. (INTERPRETIVE)

(TRADITIONAL)

　　有一天幾個朋友討論選專業的事。小王說他的父母一直想讓他畢業以後念醫學院。小林說她對工學院很有興趣，可是她父母覺得還是學醫最好。小白說爸爸媽媽不管他，他學什麼專業都可以。小白開始想選歷史專業，可是為了跟女朋友小林在一起，也考慮上醫學院。小張聽了以後就說："你們大家都學醫，那我只好學'生病專業'了。要不然，將來你們這麼多醫生到哪兒去找病人啊？"

(SIMPLIFIED)

　　有一天几个朋友讨论选专业的事。小王说他的父母一直想让他毕业以后念医学院。小林说她对工学院很有兴趣，可是她父母觉得还是学医最好。小白说爸爸妈妈不管他，他学什么专业都可以。小白开始想选历史专业，可是为了跟女朋友小林在一起，也考虑上医学院。小张听了以后就说："你们大家都学医，那我只好学'生病专业'了。要不然，将来你们这么多医生到哪儿去找病人啊？"

Questions (True/False):

( ) 1. 小王的父母不在乎他選什麼專業。
     小王的父母不在乎他选什么专业。

( ) 2. 小林覺得學工比學醫有意思。
     小林觉得学工比学医有意思。

( ) 3. 小林的父母覺得她上醫學院比較合適。
     小林的父母觉得她上医学院比较合适。

( ) 4. 小白的父母希望他學歷史。
     小白的父母希望他学历史。

( ) 5. 小張身體不好，常常生病。
     小张身体不好，常常生病。

( ) 6. 小張覺得學醫的人太多了。
     小张觉得学医的人太多了。

**D.** Look at the photo and answer the question in English. (INTERPRETIVE)

What college/school is this?_____

**E.** Look at the degree certificate issued by a mainland Chinese college and answer the questions in English. (INTERPRETIVE)

學生 李大成 系　　授予 文 學學士學位

江蘇武進人，一九八二年

十一月生。在上海外國語學院

校（院）　英 語　系

　　　英 語　專業

修業四年，成績及格，准予

畢業。經審核符合《中華人

民共和國學位條例》規定，

校（院）長　學位評定委員會主席

2003 年 7 月10日

證書編號：

学生 李大成 系　　授予 文 学学士学位

江苏武进人，一九八二年

十一月生。在上海外国语学院

校（院）　英 语 系

　　　英 语 专业

修业四年，成绩及格，准予

毕业。经审核符合《中华人

民共和国学位条例》规定，

校（院）长　学位评定委员会主席

2003 年 7 月10日

证书编号：

Questions:

**1.** What is the degree recipient's name?

_____

**2.** What is his date of birth?

_____

**3.** What is the name of the college?

_____

**4.** What is the degree recipient's major?

_____

**5.** How long is the degree program?

_____

**6.** What degree was awarded?

_____

**7.** What role does 謝童燵 serve at the college?

_____

**8.** When was the degree awarded?

_____

**F.** 這是一個報紙廣告。你能申請這些學校嗎？你想申請嗎？
為什麼?
这是一个报纸广告。你能申请这些学校吗？你想申请吗？
为什么? (INTERPRETIVE AND PRESENTATIONAL)

_____

_____

_____

_____

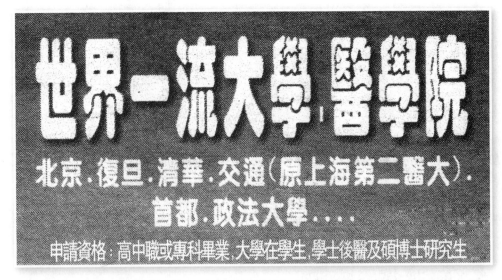

## IV. Writing and Grammar Exercises

### A. Building Characters

Form a character by combining the given components as instructed. Then write a word, a phrase, or a short sentence in which that character appears.

1. 上邊一個"田"，下邊一個"介紹"的"介"
   上边一个"田"，下边一个"介绍"的"介"，
   是 _____ 的 _____ 。

2. 左邊一個提手旁，右邊一個"受不了"的"受"
   左边一个提手旁，右边一个"受不了"的"受"，
   是 _____ 的 _____ 。

**3.** 左邊一個言字旁，右邊一個 "寸"
左边一个言字旁，右边一个 "寸"，
是 _____ 的 _____。

**4.** 上邊一個 "打折" 的 "折"，下邊一個 "口"
上边一个 "打折" 的 "折"，下边一个 "口"，
是 _____ 的 _____。

**B.** Complete the sentences using 就是 or 只是.

As the saying goes, you can't have everything. What prevents the following scenarios from being perfect?

EXAMPLE:

這條運動褲質量好，價錢便宜，　(style)
这条运动裤质量好，价钱便宜，

→ 這條運動褲質量好，價錢便宜，就是樣子不太好看。
这条运动裤质量好，价钱便宜，就是样子不太好看。

**1.** 中國歷史課很有意思，老師也很好，　(amount of homework)
中国历史课很有意思，老师也很好，

→ _____。

**2.** 夏天去上海學中文，時間沒問題，那裏我也有很多
朋友，　(affordability)

夏天去上海学中文，时间没问题，那里我也有很多
朋友，

→ _____。

**3.** 當醫生很好，能幫很多人，賺很多錢，　(leisure time)
当医生很好，能帮很多人，赚很多钱，

→ _____。

**C.** Based on your own situation or the stories from the Textbook, fill in the blanks with the correct resultative complements and answer the questions.

EXAMPLE:

> **A:** 昨天的功課你做<u>完</u>了嗎？
> 昨天的功课你做<u>完</u>了吗？
>
> **B:** <u>昨天的功課我做完了</u>。or <u>昨天的功課我沒做完</u>。
> <u>昨天的功课我做完了</u>。or <u>昨天的功课我没做完</u>。

**1. A:** 今天老師上課說的話你聽_____了嗎？
今天老师上课说的话你听_____了吗？

**B:** _____。

**2. A:** 張天明買_____他要的運動服了嗎？
张天明买_____他要的运动服了吗？

**B:** _____。

**3. A:** 李哲下學期的課選_____了嗎？
李哲下学期的课选_____了吗？

**B:** _____。

**D.** Complete the following dialogues using 肯定.

EXAMPLE:

> **A:** 已經這麼晚了，他還會來嗎？
> 已经这么晚了，他还会来吗？
>
> **B:** <u>他肯定不會來了</u>，我們別等了。
> <u>他肯定不会来了</u>，我们别等了。

**1. A:** 他下個學期會搬到校外去嗎？
他下个学期会搬到校外去吗？

**B:** _____，他已經找好房子了。
_____，他已经找好房子了。

**2. A:** 小張大學畢業以後，打算工作還是念研究生？

小张大学毕业以后，打算工作还是念研究生？

**B:** _____，他早就找到工作了。

**3. A:** 他明年五月畢得了業嗎？

他明年五月毕得了业吗？

**B:** 他還少三個學分，明年五月_____。

他还少三个学分，明年五月_____。

**E.** Based on your own situation, answer the following questions using 至於/至于.

**1. A:** 你覺得你今天穿的衣服大小、長短怎麼樣？樣子呢？

你觉得你今天穿的衣服大小、长短怎么样？样子呢？

**B:** _____。

**2. A:** 你家附近購物中心的東西質量怎麼樣？價錢呢？

你家附近购物中心的东西质量怎么样？价钱呢？

**B:** _____。

**3. A:** 你的大學的政治系、歷史系、經濟系怎麼樣？

你的大学的政治系、历史系、经济系怎么样？

**B:** _____。

**F.** Use 至於/至于 to complete the tasks.

**1.** Your younger brother is trying to decide on a major and is asking for your help comparing the following two possibilities.

請你談談電腦和金融這兩個專業。

请你谈谈电脑和金融这两个专业。

_____

_____

_____

_____

**2.** Your roommate is thinking about whether to stay in the dorm or move off campus next year. She is asking you for your advice.

談一談住在校內和住在校外的好處和壞處。

談一談住在校內和住在校外的好處和壞處。

谈一谈住在校内和住在校外的好处和坏处。

_____

_____

_____

_____

**3.** You are a salesperson. A customer is examining a sports outfit. You try to be helpful by talking about different aspects of the outfit, including its brand, color, material, price, etc.

_____

_____

_____

_____

**G.** Complete the following dialogues using 另外 (the other).

EXAMPLE:

**A:** 你的同屋都是新生嗎？

你的同屋都是新生吗？

**B:** 我有三個同屋，兩個新生，<u>另外一個是老生</u>。

我有三个同屋，两个新生，<u>另外一个是老生</u>。

**1. A:** 這附近有幾家購物中心？離這兒遠嗎？

这附近有几家购物中心？离这儿远吗？

**B:** 有兩家。一家很近，_____。

**2. A:** 我們放三天假，你打算做什麼？

我们放三天假，你打算做什么？

**B:** 我打算一天洗衣服，_____。

**3. A:** 他的三個弟弟都大學畢業了吧？

他的三个弟弟都大学毕业了吧？

**B:** 他的大弟弟已經畢業了，_____。

他的大弟弟已经毕业了，_____。

**H.** Complete the following brief dialogues using 另外 (besides).

EXAMPLE:

**A:** 這層樓有什麼？

这层楼有什么？

**B:** 這層樓有洗衣機和烘乾機，<u>另外還有電腦</u>。

这层楼有洗衣机和烘干机，<u>另外还有电脑</u>。

**1. A:** 你這學期上什麼課？

你这学期上什么课？

**B:** 我這學期上中文，_____。

我这学期上中文，_____。

**2. A:** 張天明、麗莎、柯林和林雪梅四個人去中國飯館吃飯，點了些什麼菜？

张天明、丽莎、柯林和林雪梅三个人去中国饭馆吃饭，点了些什么菜？

**B:** 他們點了芥蘭牛肉，_____。

他们点了芥兰牛肉，_____。

**3. A:** 林雪梅和麗莎需要買些什麼日用品？

林雪梅和丽莎需要买些什么日用品？

**B:** 她們需要買衛生紙、牙膏，_____。

她们需要买卫生纸、牙膏，_____。

**I.** Use 要麼…要麼…/要么…要么… to complete the following dialogues.

**1. A:** 這個週末你打算做什麼?
這个周末你打算做什么?

**B:** _____ 。

**2. A:** 你今天晚飯想吃什麼?
你今天晚饭想吃什么?

**B:** _____ 。

**3. A:** 你希望媽媽送給你什麼生日禮物?
你希望妈妈送给你什么生日礼物?

**B:** _____ 。

**J.** Complete the following dialogues using 跟…打交道.

EXAMPLE:

**A:** 你為什麼不念醫學院?          (patients)
你为什么不念医学院?

**B:** <u>因為我不願意跟病人打交道</u>。
<u>因为我不愿意跟病人打交道</u>。

**1. A:** 你為什麼不當售貨員了?                    (money, customers)
你为什么不当售货员了?

**B:** _____ 。

**2. A:** 你的專業是金融，這份工作對你很合適，怎麼不申請?
                                                                (numbers)
你的专业是金融，这份工作对你很合适，怎么不申请?

**B:** _____ 。

**3. A:** 快開學了，學校需要一些老生幫新生搬進宿舍，你的同屋為什麼不願意幫忙？                                    (freshmen)

快开学了，学校需要一些老生帮新生搬进宿舍，你的同屋为什么不愿意帮忙？

**B:** _____ 。

**K.** Complete the following sentences using 其實/其实.

EXAMPLE:

我的同學都覺得這次考試有一點兒難，<u>其實這次考試不太難</u>。

我的同学都觉得这次考试有一点儿难，<u>其实这次考试不太难</u>。

1. 大家都覺得那個飯館的菜很地道，_____ 。

   大家都觉得那个饭馆的菜很地道，_____ 。

2. 很多人都覺得住在校外比較好，_____ 。

   很多人都觉得住在校外比较好，_____ 。

3. 最近有一些報紙文章說中國菜太油，_____ 。

   最近有一些报纸文章说中国菜太油，_____ 。

**L.** Translate the following sentences using 其實/其实.(PRESENTATIONAL)

1. Everyone thought she was Chinese. She's actually Japanese.

   _____

2. I thought the food in the dorm would be terrible. Actually, it was not as bad as I thought.

   _____

3. I don't listen to my parents too much. But as a matter of fact, what they say does make sense.

   _____

4. Many college freshmen thought it would be more economical to rent an apartment. In fact, it was not necessarily so.

   _____

**M.** Translate the following conversations into Chinese. (PRESENTATIONAL)

**1. A:** Have you finished choosing your courses for next semester?

_____

**B:** Yes, I've finished. I've chosen Chinese, Chemistry, Economics, and World History. How about you? Have you finished choosing?

_____

**A:** I also want to take Chinese and Chemistry. As for the other two, I haven't thought it through. I'll see my advisor tomorrow. I'd like to ask her.

_____

**2. A:** This sweatsuit is really nice.

_____

**B:** It is very nice, but it's just that the price is too high.

_____

**A:** Actually, I'd also like to save money. But other sweatsuits are too poorly made.

_____

**B:** Are you telling me that no matter how expensive it is, you'll buy it?

_____

**A:** Either you buy things of good quality or you don't buy anything at all. As for price, I don't care.

_____

**N.** Translate the following passages into Chinese. (PRESENTATIONAL)

**1.** My major is computer science. I am graduating next year. But I don't have any work experience, so I've decided to intern at a computer company this winter break.

_____

_____

_____

**2.** Little Lin spent a lot of time preparing for exams and writing papers this week. He felt it was too much to bear. He hoped he wouldn't have to worry about studying this weekend and could relax a little.

_____

_____

_____

**3.** My older brother plans to go to graduate school after he graduates next semester. He says he will study either engineering or medicine. My parents hope that he will study computer science and make a lot of money in the future. They know that he could make even more money in the future if he chooses to go to medical school. However, they don't want to make him deal with patients all day long.

_____

_____

_____

_____

**O.** Write a composition about your current academic studies, including information such as: courses you have taken in the past, courses you are currently taking, credits you need to graduate, your major, the reason you chose your major (if you do not have a major yet, what you hope to major in), your parents' influence on your choice of major if applicable, your outlook on graduate work or job prospects after graduating from college, etc. (PRESENTATIONAL)

## P. Storytelling (PRESENTATIONAL)

Write a story in Chinese based on the four cartoons below. Make sure that your story has a beginning, a middle, and an end. Also make sure that the transition from one picture to the next is smooth and logical.

**1**

**2**

**3**

**4**

# Let's Review (LESSONS 1–5)

## I. How Good Is Your Pronunciation?

Write down the correct pronunciation and tones of the following short sentences in *pinyin*, and use a tape recorder or computer to record them. Hand in the recording to your teacher if asked. Then translate each sentence into English. (INTERPRETIVE)

**1.** 學校離家很遠。
學校離家很远。

_____

_____

**2.** 學生公寓很安全。
学生公寓很安全。

_____

_____

**3.** 住在校外的好處不少。
住在校外的好处不少。

_____

_____

**4.** 這棟樓比較舊。
这栋楼比较旧。

_____

_____

**5.** 靠窗戶擺著一台洗衣機。
靠窗户摆着一台洗衣机。

_____

_____

**6.** 過馬路別着急。
过马路别着急。

_____

_____

**7.** 那個留學生是研究生。
那个留学生是研究生。

_____

_____

**8.** 做魚紅燒不如清蒸。
做鱼红烧不如清蒸。

_____

_____

**9.** 這雞又油又鹹。
这鸡又油又咸。

_____

_____

**10.** 這條牛仔褲的質量好。
这条牛仔裤的质量好。

_____

_____

**11.** 你的購物標準是什麼？
你的购物标准是什么？

_____

_____

**12.** 她非買純棉的衣服不可。
她非买纯棉的衣服不可。

_____

_____

**13.** 無論買什麼都得加稅。
无论买什么都得加税。

_____

_____

**14.** 我考慮選金融做專業。
我考虑选金融做专业。

_____

_____

**15.** 我建議這件事明天再討論。
我建议这件事明天再讨论。

_____

_____

## II. Put Your Chinese to Good Use! (PRESENTATIONAL)

Complete the following tasks in Chinese.

Imagine that you are going to China. Before you go, find out if you know enough Chinese to get by:

**A.** Suppose you are in a grocery store in China. What food items and cooking ingredients can you name without looking at your textbook? List them here:

_____

_____

_____

_____

_____

_____

_____

_____

**B.** Suppose you are in a Chinese restaurant. What dishes can you name without looking them up? List them here:

**1.** Meat dishes: _____

**2.** Vegetarian dishes: _____

**3.** Soups: _____

**4.** Spicy dishes: _____

**5.** Beverages: _____

**C.** Suppose you are in a convenience store in China getting some daily necessities. What items can you name without asking your Chinese friends? List them here:

_____

_____

_____

_____

_____

_____

_____

**D.** Suppose you are shopping in an apparel store in China. What pieces of clothing can you ask the salesperson to show you? List them here:

_____

_____

_____

_____

_____

_____

_____

**E.** Suppose you are reading the academic directory of a Chinese university. What departments/ schools can you identify? List them here:

_____

_____

_____

_____

_____

_____

_____

## III. Getting to Know You! (PRESENTATIONAL)

Make lists in Chinese.

**A.** Information that you want people to know about you when you first meet:

_____

_____

_____

_____

_____

**B.** Your opinions on on-campus and off-campus living:

On–campus living

Pros                                    Cons

_____    _____

_____    _____

_____    _____

_____    _____

_____    _____


Off–campus living

Pros                                    Cons

_____    _____

_____    _____

_____    _____

_____    _____

_____    _____

**C.** Your dietary restrictions and/or preferences:

| Restrictions | Preferences |
|---|---|
| _____ | _____ |
| _____ | _____ |
| _____ | _____ |
| _____ | _____ |
| _____ | _____ |

**D.** Your preferences and criteria when shopping for clothes, with the most important listed as #1:

1. _____

2. _____

3. _____

4. _____

5. _____

**E.** Academic courses and additional career planning resources that you think may help your future job prospects:

```
_____

_____

_____

_____

_____

_____

_____
```

After you have finished your own lists, interview a classmate about his/her opinions on these topics.

# IV. Express Yourself! (PRESENTATIONAL)

Based on, but not limited to, the information you have provided in Parts II and III, present an oral report or write a short essay in Chinese in response to each of the following questions.

**A.** What advice would you give if asked whether it would be better to live on campus or off campus?

**B.** How would you describe the interior and the surroundings of your ideal living quarters?

**C.** Suppose your personal chef is to prepare a Chinese meal for you. What instructions would you give him or her?

**D.** Suppose your personal assistant is going to shop for a new outfit for you. What instructions would you give him or her?

**E.** Suppose you are a career counselor. What advice would you give to students to help them be more competitive in the job market after graduation?

第六課　　男朋友女朋友

第六课　　男朋友女朋友

# I. Listening Comprehension

## A. Textbook Content (INTERPRETIVE)

Listen to the recording for the Textbook and answer the questions in English.

**1.** When did Zhang Tianming and Lisa first meet each other?

_____

**2.** Why is Xuemei visiting Lisa this evening?

_____

**3.** What has happened between Zhang Tianming and Lisa recently?

_____

**4.** What is Xuemei's reply to Lisa?

_____

**5.** What does Xuemei say to Lisa to make Lisa feel she's not alone?

_____

## B. Workbook Dialogue (INTERPRETIVE)

Listen to the recording for the Workbook and answer the questions.

Questions (True/False):

( )　**1.** The two speakers are in front of a movie theater.

( )　**2.** When Tianming called, he had been in front of a movie theater for twenty minutes.

( )　**3.** Lisa was about to call Tianming when she received the call from him.

( )　**4.** Lisa lost track of time because she was watching a concert on TV.

( )　**5.** Lisa arrived at the movie theater around 7:55.

( )　**6.** Lisa couldn't find Tianming because there were too many people there.

( )　**7.** Finally Tianming realized that he was not in a position to forgive Lisa.

## C. Workbook Narratives

**1.** Listen to the recording for the Workbook and answer the questions in English. (INTERPRETIVE)

**a.** Why was Little Wang in a bad mood yesterday?

_____

**b.** Why did his friends invite Little Wang to play ball?

_____

**c.** What made Little Wang's girlfriend angry?

_____

**d.** Do you think Little Wang cares about his girlfriend?

_____

**2.** Listen to the recording for the Workbook and answer the questions in English. (INTERPRETIVE)

**a.** In what ways is Little Li different from her boyfriend?

_____

**b.** How would you describe Little Li's relationship with her boyfriend?

_____

**c.** Do their different hobbies affect their relationship adversely? Why or why not?

_____

**3.** Listen to the recording for the Workbook and answer the questions in English. (INTERPRETIVE)

**a.** How would you describe Xiaoming?

_____

**b.** In what way is Xiaoming different from his mother?

_____

**c.** Why is Xiaoming's mother so concerned?

_____

## D. Workbook Listening Rejoinder (INTERPERSONAL)

In this section, you will hear two people talking. After hearing the first speaker, select the best from the four possible responses given by the second speaker.

_____

## II. Speaking Exercises

**A.** Practice asking and answering the following questions. (INTERPERSONAL)

1. 什麼事會讓你心情不好?
   什么事会让你心情不好?

2. 什麼事會讓你着急?
   什么事会让你着急?

3. 什麼事會讓你生氣?
   什么事会让你生气?

4. 你對什麼有興趣?
   你对什么有兴趣?

5. 你覺得班上同學誰的性格比較開朗?
   你觉得班上同学谁的性格比较开朗?

6. 你家裏誰常常忘這忘那,丟三拉四?
   你家里谁常常忘这忘那,丢三拉四?

**B.** Practice speaking on the following topics. (PRESENTATIONAL)

1. 請談一談自己的興趣和愛好。
   请谈一谈自己的兴趣和爱好。

2. 請談一談你選男朋友/女朋友的標準。
   请谈一谈你选男朋友/女朋友的标准。

3. Your friend is trying to persuade you to go on a blind date with someone, so he or she tries to present the person in the best possible light, telling you about the person's hobbies and interests, special skills, personality, etc. You, however, are wary. You have a lot of questions about that person that you would like your friend to answer.

# III. Reading Comprehension

## A. Building Words

Complete this section by writing the characters, the *pinyin*, and the English equivalent of each new word formed. Guess the meaning before you use a dictionary to confirm.

**1.** "下雪" 的 "雪" + "籃球" 的 "球"
   "下雪" 的 "雪" + "篮球" 的 "球"

   → _____ _____ _____
     new word      *pinyin*      English

**2.** "背景" 的 "背" + "電影院" 的 "影"
   "背景" 的 "背" + "电影院" 的 "影"

   → _____ _____ _____

**3.** "打球" 的 "打" + "吵架" 的 "架"

   → _____ _____ _____

**4.** "道歉" 的 "歉" + "意思" 的 "意"

   → _____ _____ _____

**5.** "記仇" 的 "仇" + "中國人" 的 "人"
   "记仇" 的 "仇" + "中国人" 的 "人"

   → _____ _____ _____

**6.** "丟三拉四" 的 "丟" + "臉圓圓的" 的 "臉"
   "丢三拉四" 的 "丢" + "脸圆圆的" 的 "脸"

   → _____ _____ _____

**B.** Fill in the blanks with the phrases provided.

想來想去　走來走去　找來找去　考慮來考慮去　等來等去
想来想去　走来走去　找来找去　考虑来考虑去　等来等去

1. 小梅病了，她的男朋友來看她，可是醫生正在給她檢查，不能進去。他在外邊着急地_____，不知道什麼時候可以進去。

   小梅病了，她的男朋友来看她，可是医生正在给她检查，不能进去。他在外边着急地_____，不知道什么时候可以进去。

2. 老王常常忘這忘那，東西亂放，昨天鑰匙不見了，_____，原來在冰箱裏。

   老王常常忘这忘那，东西乱放，昨天钥匙不见了，_____，原来在冰箱里。

3. 大家約好了一起坐地鐵去看演唱會，可是_____，小林還不來，大家都很生氣。

   大家约好了一起坐地铁去看演唱会，可是_____，小林还不来，大家都很生气。

4. 這個問題很大，公司裏的人_____還是沒辦法解決。

   这个问题很大，公司里的人_____还是没办法解决。

5. 表哥快大學畢業了，_____，最後決定找工作不念研究生了。

   表哥快大学毕业了，_____，最后决定找工作不念研究生了。

**C.** Read the passage and answer the questions. (INTERPRETIVE)

(TRADITIONAL)

張天明的父母性格都很開朗，兩個人一直相處得很好，很少吵架。他們都很愛交朋友，興趣也差不多一樣，比如他們都喜歡聽音樂、跳舞。他們也都愛旅行，去過世界很多地方。另外，兩個人都喜歡看電視。不過張先生是個籃球迷，喜歡看籃球賽。張太太對籃球一點興趣都沒有，但特別喜歡看滑冰比賽。晚上的電視如果又有籃球比賽又有滑冰比賽的話，張太太就只好讓張先生看，自己給朋友打電話聊天。可是有的時候張先生為了讓太太高興，也只好不看籃球賽，陪太太一起看滑冰。難怪他們兩個人很少吵架。

張天明昨天晚上看電視的時候想到爸爸媽媽看電視的事，就給爸爸打電話，讓爸爸給媽媽再買一個電視，送給媽媽當生日禮物。

(SIMPLIFIED)

张天明的父母性格都很开朗，两个人一直相处得很好，很少吵架。他们都很爱交朋友，兴趣也差不多一样，比如他们都喜欢听音乐、跳舞。他们也都爱旅行，去过世界很多地方。另外，两个人都喜欢看电视。不过张先生是个篮球迷，喜欢看篮球赛。张太太对篮球一点兴趣都没有，但特别喜欢看滑冰比赛。晚上的电视如果又有篮球比赛又有滑冰比赛的话，张太太就只好让张先生看，自己给朋友打电话聊天。可是有的时候张先生为了让太太高兴，也只好不看篮球赛，陪太太一起看滑冰。难怪他们两个人很少吵架。

张天明昨天晚上看电视的时候想到爸爸妈妈看电视的事，就给爸爸打电话，让爸爸给妈妈再买一个电视，送给妈妈当生日礼物。

Questions (True/False):

( ) **1.** Mr. and Mrs. Zhang are more similar than different in terms of personality and interests.

( ) **2.** Mr. and Mrs. Zhang like to watch different TV programs.

( ) **3.** They like to travel, listen to music, dance, watch TV, and hang out with friends.

( ) **4.** Mr. Zhang makes Mrs. Zhang call her friends whenever there's a basketball game on TV.

( )　**5.** Mr. Zhang sometimes watches ice skating to make his wife happy.

( )　**6.** The secret of their successful marriage is that they have two TVs.

**D.** Read the passage and complete the task. (INTERPRETIVE)

(TRADITIONAL)

　　小白的父親一直希望小白在大學好好學習，不要交男朋友。可是小白上個星期打電話回家，告訴父親她交男朋友了，他叫湯姆。小白説，雖然湯姆的文化背景跟她不一樣，可是性格很開朗，長得也挺帥。白先生聽了決定自己去看看。昨天是星期六，白先生開車來到小白上學的城市，約好十二點半在一家中國餐館跟湯姆見面，可是湯姆一點鐘才到。小白很着急，一問，才知道他跑到一家日本餐館去了。白先生很生氣。他覺得湯姆這樣馬虎，跟小白不會相處得很好。可是湯姆不停地道歉，態度特別好，白先生覺得湯姆可能還是真心的，於是就同意他們兩個人交朋友。

(SIMPLIFIED)

　　小白的父亲一直希望小白在大学好好学习，不要交男朋友。可是小白上个星期打电话回家，告诉父亲她交男朋友了，他叫汤姆。小白说，虽然汤姆的文化背景跟她不一样，可是性格很开朗，长得也挺帅。白先生听了决定自己去看看。昨天是星期六，白先生开车来到小白上学的城市，约好十二点半在一家中国餐馆跟汤姆见面，可是汤姆一点钟才到。小白很着急，一问，才知道他跑到一家日本餐馆去了。白先生很生气。他觉得汤姆这样马虎，跟小白不会相处得很好。可是汤姆不停地道歉，态度特别好，白先生觉得汤姆可能还是真心的，于是就同意他们两个人交朋友。

Tom has been evaluated by Little Bai and Mr. Bai. List in English the positive aspects about Tom in the thumbs-up column, and the negative in the thumbs-down column.

**E.** Fill in the blanks with either 的, 得, or 地.

(TRADITIONAL)

　　小王上個星期跟指導教授約好昨天上午九點討論選課_____事。可是他把這件事忘_____一乾二淨。今天中午在餐廳碰見指導教授，小王才想起來，他就不停_____給教授道歉。教授生氣_____看了看小王，一句話也沒説，很快_____走出了餐廳。

(SIMPLIFIED)

　　小王上个星期跟指导教授约好昨天上午九点讨论选课_____事。可是他把这件事忘_____一干二净。今天中午在餐厅碰见指导教授，小王才想起来，他就不停_____给教授道歉。教授生气_____看了看小王，一句话也没说，很快_____走出了餐厅。

**F.** Answer the questions in English based on this movie theater's advertisement. (INTERPRETIVE)

近期活動
1、週一咖啡日；週二電影全天半價；週一週三爆米花特價賣；週四觀影女士半價；週五、六夜場通宵連放；
2、持本人老年證、本人學生證（23週歲以下）觀影半價；
3、每天中午12:30前22:00後觀影半價。

近期活动
1、周一咖啡日；周二电影全天半价；周一周三爆米花特价卖；周四观影女士半价；周五、六夜场通宵连放；
2、持本人老年证、本人学生证（23周岁以下）观影半价；
3、每天中午12:30前22:00后观影半价。

**1.** Which day of the week would you go there for a movie? Why?

_____

**2.** What discount does the movie theater offer to senior citizens?

_____

**3.** What discount does it offer for a morning show?

_____

**G.** Take a look at this personal ad from an online dating service and answer the questions. The person's name and birthday have been changed in order to protect the privacy of the individual. (INTERPRETIVE)

| 姓名 | 王小梅 | 星座 | 雙子座 |
|---|---|---|---|
| 性別 | | 出生年月 | 1983 年 6 月 14 日 |
| 身高 | 165 cm | 體重 | 48 kg |
| 所在城市 | 北京 | 老家 | 海淀 |
| 國籍 | 中國 | 血型 | O 型 |
| 婚姻狀況 | 未婚 | 體型 | 保密 |
| 休息日 | 雙休六日 | 月收入 | 保密 |
| 學歷 | 大學專科 | 畢業學校 | 北京醫科大學 |
| 兄妹情況 | 兄妹兩人以上 | 專業 | 眼科 |
| 工作情況 | 在職 | 從事職業 | 醫生 |
| 吸煙 | 不吸 | | |
| 喝酒 | 偶爾 | | |
| 住房 | 與父母同住 | 汽車 | 有買車計劃 |
| 擅長(愛好) | 聽音樂、跑步 | | |
| 性格自介 | 活潑開朗,外向,溫柔體貼,不拘小節,害羞,老實,敏感,快言快語 | | |

| 姓名 | 王小梅 | 星座 | 双子座 |
|---|---|---|---|
| 性別 | | 出生年月 | 1983 年 6 月 14 日 |
| 身高 | 165 cm | 体重 | 48 kg |
| 所在城市 | 北京 | 老家 | 海淀 |
| 国籍 | 中国 | 血型 | O 型 |
| 婚姻状况 | 未婚 | 体型 | 保密 |
| 休息日 | 双休六日 | 月收入 | 保密 |
| 学历 | 大学专科 | 毕业学校 | 北京医科大学 |
| 兄妹情况 | 兄妹两人以上 | 专业 | 眼科 |
| 工作情况 | 在职 | 从事职业 | 医生 |
| 吸烟 | 不吸 | | |
| 喝酒 | 偶尔 | | |
| 住房 | 与父母同住 | 汽车 | 有买车计划 |
| 擅长（爱好） | 听音乐、跑步 | | |
| 性格自介 | 活泼开朗,外向,温柔体贴,不拘小节,害羞,老实,敏感,快言快语 | | |

Questions: (True/False)

( ) **1.** She lives in Beijing with her parents.

( ) **2.** She doesn't have any siblings.

( ) **3.** She's never been married.

( ) **4.** She graduated from a medical school.

( ) **5.** She gets one day off from work every week.

( ) **6.** She owns a car.

( ) **7.** She considers herself outgoing.

# IV. Writing and Grammar Exercises

## A. Building Characters

Form a character by combining the given components as instructed. Then write a word, a phrase, or a short sentence in which that character appears.

1. 左邊一個 "木"，右邊一個 "目"
   左边一个 "木"，右边一个 "目"，
   是 _____ 的 _____ 。

2. 上邊一個 "北"，下邊一個 "月"
   上边一个 "北"，下边一个 "月"，
   是 _____ 的 _____ 。

3. 上邊一個 "日"，下邊一個 "北京" 的 "京"
   上边一个 "日"，下边一个 "北京" 的 "京"，
   是 _____ 的 _____ 。

4. 左邊一個 "口"，右邊一個 "合適" 的 "合"
   左边一个 "口"，右边一个 "合适" 的 "合"，
   是 _____ 的 _____ 。

**B.** Clear up the confusion surrounding the main characters in the textbook by first asking questions using 到底, and then answering based on the texts.

EXAMPLE:

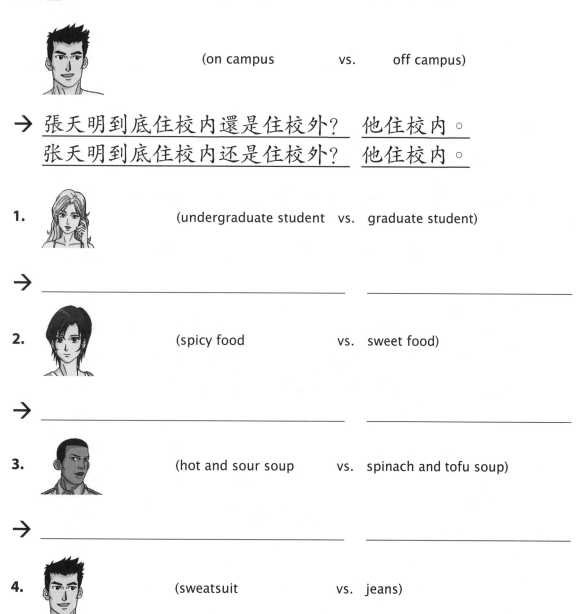

(on campus　　　vs.　　off campus)

→ 張天明到底住校內還是住校外？　他住校內。
　　张天明到底住校内还是住校外？　他住校内。

1.　　　　　　　(undergraduate student　vs.　graduate student)

→ _____　_____

2.　　　　　　　(spicy food　　　vs.　sweet food)

→ _____　_____

3.　　　　　　　(hot and sour soup　　vs.　spinach and tofu soup)

→ _____　_____

4.　　　　　　　(sweatsuit　　　vs.　jeans)

→ _____　_____

5.　　　　　　　(finding a job　　vs.　going to graduate school)

→ _____　_____

**C.** Paraphrase the following sentences using 原來/原来 (originally).

EXAMPLE:

三年前我認識他的時候，他在學日文。過了幾個月就
不學了。

三年前我认识他的时候，他在学日文。过了几个月就
不学了。

→ <u>他原來學日文，後來不學了</u>。
<u>他原来学日文，后来不学了</u>。

1. 他上高中的時候，常常運動，上大學以後，就不運動
了。

他上高中的时候，常常运动，上大学以后，就不运动
了。

→ _____。

2. 他小時候常常吃肉，現在只吃素菜，不吃肉了。
他小时候常常吃肉，现在只吃素菜，不吃肉了。

→ _____。

3. 小柯想點清蒸魚，但是服務員說賣完了，只好叫了三十
個餃子。

小柯想点清蒸鱼，但是服务员说卖完了，只好叫了三十
个饺子。

→ _____。

**D.** Did any of the main characters' experiences catch you by surprise? Use 原來/原来 (as it turns out) to describe your realization.

EXAMPLE:

我以為張天明是在大學認識的麗莎，<u>原來他們在高中的</u>
<u>時候就認識了</u>。

我以为张天明是在大学认识的丽莎，<u>原来他们在高中的</u>
<u>时候就认识了</u>。

**1.** 我以為柯林是大學一年級的新生，＿＿＿＿＿＿＿＿＿＿。

　　我以为柯林是大学一年级的新生，＿＿＿＿＿＿＿＿＿＿。

**2.** 我以為張天明對金融很有興趣，＿＿＿＿＿＿＿＿＿。

　　我以为张天明对金融很有兴趣，＿＿＿＿＿＿＿＿＿。

**3.** 我以為麗莎是個球迷，＿＿＿＿＿＿＿＿＿＿＿＿。

　　我以为丽莎是个球迷，＿＿＿＿＿＿＿＿＿＿＿＿。

**4.** 我以為林雪梅已經把她交男朋友的事兒告訴家裏了，

＿＿＿＿＿＿＿＿＿＿＿＿＿＿＿＿＿＿＿＿＿。

　　我以为林雪梅已经把她交男朋友的事儿告诉家里了，

＿＿＿＿＿＿＿＿＿＿＿＿＿＿＿＿＿＿＿＿＿。

**5.** 我以為李哲有工作經驗，＿＿＿＿＿＿＿＿＿＿＿。

　　我以为李哲有工作经验，＿＿＿＿＿＿＿＿＿＿＿。

**E.** Translate the following sentences into Chinese. (PRESENTATIONAL)

**1.** I thought he didn't like the sweet and sour fish I made. As it turned out, he was allergic to fish.

＿＿＿＿＿＿＿＿＿＿＿＿＿＿＿＿＿＿＿＿＿＿

＿＿＿＿＿＿＿＿＿＿＿＿＿＿＿＿＿＿＿＿＿＿

**2.** In terms of hobbies, my roommate and I both like singing and dancing. But in terms of academic studies, I like to deal with numbers, but she doesn't.

＿＿＿＿＿＿＿＿＿＿＿＿＿＿＿＿＿＿＿＿＿＿

＿＿＿＿＿＿＿＿＿＿＿＿＿＿＿＿＿＿＿＿＿＿

**3.** Why not give the taxi company a call? You never know, perhaps they have found your keys.

＿＿＿＿＿＿＿＿＿＿＿＿＿＿＿＿＿＿＿＿＿＿

＿＿＿＿＿＿＿＿＿＿＿＿＿＿＿＿＿＿＿＿＿＿

**4.** My roommate was especially busy yesterday afternoon. He was cooking one minute, doing laundry the next, and tidying up the room, too.

＿＿＿＿＿＿＿＿＿＿＿＿＿＿＿＿＿＿＿＿＿＿

＿＿＿＿＿＿＿＿＿＿＿＿＿＿＿＿＿＿＿＿＿＿

**F.** Translate the following dialogues into Chinese. (PRESENTATIONAL)

**1. A:** How is your boyfriend?

   **B:** Don't bring it up. He doesn't care about me at all.

   **A:** What happened? Does he have another girlfriend?

   **B:** No. Every day all he wants to do is play basketball with his friends. He's only got basketball on his mind. Last Saturday evening we had a date to see a movie. Who knew? He played basketball with his friends all night long and totally forgot about the movie. How could I not have gotten angry?

   **A:** No wonder you were mad. Next time, ask him out on a date to watch a basketball game. Show up half an hour late. Keep him waiting.

   **B:** That's a good idea.

   _____

   _____

   _____

   _____

   _____

   _____

   _____

**2. A:** How is your boyfriend?

   **B:** Not bad, just very careless.

   **A:** Careless in what way?

   **B:** He often forgets this or that, or leaves things behind. Last month for my birthday he bought me a book, but he didn't realize until he was back in the dorm that he had left it in the cab. Two nights ago he invited a friend of his to dinner. When it was time to pay, I saw he was very embarrassed. Turned out he had forgotten to bring any money or his credit card. I ended up paying.

   **A:** No wonder you said he was careless.

   _____

   _____

   _____

   _____

   _____

_____

_____

_____

_____

_____

_____

**G.** Translate the following passages into Chinese. (PRESENTATIONAL)

**1.** Something seemed to be bothering my younger sister. I asked her repeatedly what it was before she said that she had quarreled with her boyfriend Little Zhang. Little Zhang is a nice guy. He's tall and handsome, and very outgoing. What really happened between the two? It turns out that many girls like Little Zhang, and my sister thought Little Zhang liked them, too. She was not sure if Little Zhang genuinely cared about her.

_____

_____

_____

_____

_____

_____

_____

**2.** My grandma and grandpa used to fight all the time. My grandpa is a basketball fan. Whenever there is a game on TV, he has to watch it. My grandma is a fan of pop music. Whenever there is a concert on TV, she'll insist on watching it, too. But they only had one TV, so my dad bought them another TV. Grandma and Grandpa then each watched their own TV, and didn't fight anymore. But later on Grandma said that watching TV alone was no fun, and that they would like to give one of the TVs to someone else. Now I understand that although Grandma and Grandpa fought all the time, in reality they were "an old married couple, so they didn't hold grudges."

_____

_____

_____

_____

_____

_____

_____

_____

**H.** Suppose you are helping your older brother or sister place a personal ad in a magazine. The following is a personal information form that you need to help him/her fill out in order to place the ad. Fill in the blanks. (INTERPRETIVE AND PRESENTATIONAL)

### 留學人員徵婚需填表格

| 姓 名 | | 性 別 | | 出生日期 | | 民 族 | |
|---|---|---|---|---|---|---|---|
| 籍 貫 | | 身 高 | | 相 貌 | | 學 歷 | |
| 愛 好 | | 職 業 | | 護照號 | | 所在國 | |
| 居留身份 | | | | 婚姻狀況 | | | |
| 有無子女 | | | | 身體狀況 | | | |
| 通訊地址 | | | | | | 電 話 | |
| 其它情況 | | | | | | | |
| 要求對方 | | | | | | | |

### 留学人员征婚需填表格

| 姓 名 | | 性 別 | | 出生日期 | | 民 族 | |
|---|---|---|---|---|---|---|---|
| 籍 贯 | | 身 高 | | 相 貌 | | 学 历 | |
| 爱 好 | | 职 业 | | 护照号 | | 所在国 | |
| 居留身份 | | | | 婚姻状况 | | | |
| 有无子女 | | | | 身体状况 | | | |
| 通讯地址 | | | | | | 电 话 | |
| 其它情况 | | | | | | | |
| 要求对方 | | | | | | | |

**I.** List the qualities that you look for in a date, and the qualities you hope he or she doesn't have. (PRESENTATIONAL)

_____

_____

_____

_____

_____

_____

_____

_____

_____

_____

**J.** Imagine you are going to help your brother or sister send in a 90-second video clip to an online matchmaking agency. Before shooting the video, write a draft of what he or she wants to say about himself or herself and what he or she looks for in an ideal girlfriend or boyfriend. Make sure to include basic information such as his or her name, where he or she is from, education, etc., and personal traits that are important to him/her. (PRESENTATIONAL)

_____

_____

_____

_____

_____

_____

_____

_____

_____

_____

## K. Storytelling (PRESENTATIONAL)

Write a story in Chinese based on the four cartoons below. Make sure that your story has a beginning, a middle, and an end. Also make sure that the transition from one picture to the next is smooth and logical.

1

2

3

4

**7**

第七課　　電腦和網絡
第七课　　电脑和网络

# I. Listening Comprehension

## A. Textbook Content (INTERPRETIVE)

Listen to the recording for the Textbook and answer the questions in English.

**1.** Why is Zhang Tianming late for the appointment?

_____

**2.** What does Xuemei's professor think of the information on the internet?

_____

**3.** Why does Lisa tell Zhang Tianming that one can find a girlfriend online?

_____

**4.** Why does Zhang Tianming prefer email over the telephone?

_____

**5.** What does Ke Lin say about Xuemei's use of the telephone?

_____

## B. Workbook Dialogue (INTERPRETIVE)

Listen to the recording for the Workbook and answer the questions.

Questions (True/False):

( )　**1.** Tianming was online for half an hour before he started to have the stomachache.

( )　**2.** Tianming ordered the stomachache medicine online.

( )　**3.** Lisa does not consider all information on the internet to be equally reliable.

( )　**4.** In the end, Tianming may have to agree that Lisa's view of online information is not outdated after all.

( )　**5.** Zhang Tianming didn't go to a doctor for his stomachache because he couldn't wait for Lisa to take him.

## C. Workbook Narratives

1. Listen to the recording for the Workbook and answer the questions in English. (INTERPRETIVE)

   **a.** Does the speaker advocate that people should get rid of computers?

   _____

   **b.** List the five things that people do online, according to the speaker.

   _____

   **c.** According to the speaker, why are computers detrimental to people's health?

   _____

2. Listen to the recording for the Workbook and answer the questions in English. (INTERPRETIVE)

   **a.** Who is the speaker, and to whom is he speaking?

   _____

   **b.** Does the speaker encourage his audience to use the internet? Why or why not?

   _____

   **c.** What does the speaker think of the school library?

   _____

3. Listen to the recording for the Workbook and answer the questions in English. (INTERPRETIVE)

   **a.** Who is the speaker?

   _____

   **b.** What does the speaker think is the difference between email and telephone conversations?

   _____

   **c.** Why does the speaker have to try to call Tianming repeatedly today?

   _____

   **d.** How would you describe the speaker's mood?

   _____

**D. Workbook Listening Rejoinder** (INTERPERSONAL)

In this section, you will hear two people talking. After hearing the first speaker, select the best from the four possible responses given by the second speaker.

---

# II. Speaking Exercises

**A.** Practice asking and answering the following questions. (INTERPERSONAL)

**1.** 你的電腦從早到晚都開著嗎？為什麼？
   你的电脑从早到晚都开着吗？为什么？

**2.** 你每天上網差不多上多長時間？
   你每天上网差不多上多长时间？

**3.** 你上網做些什麼？
   你上网做些什么？

**4.** 你的生活離得開離不開電腦？
   你的生活离得开离不开电脑？

**5.** 要是你的朋友玩電腦玩上癮了，你會跟他説什麼？
   要是你的朋友玩电脑玩上瘾了，你会跟他说什么？

**B.** Practice speaking on the following topics. (PRESENTATIONAL)

**1.** 請談談電腦網絡給你的生活帶來了什麼好處。
   请谈谈电脑网络给你的生活带来了什么好处。

**2.** 請談談電腦網絡給你的生活帶來了什麼壞處。
   请谈谈电脑网络给你的生活带来了什么坏处。

**3.** Imagine your friend is hooked on internet games and doesn't even care about eating or sleeping, let alone having a social life. You are going to intervene and remind him or her about things that truly matter.

# III. Reading Comprehension

## A. Building Words

Complete this section by writing the characters, the *pinyin* and the English equivalent of each new word formed. Guess the meaning before you use a dictionary to confirm.

**1.** "網路" 的 "網" ＋ "電腦迷" 的 "迷"
　　"网络" 的 "网" ＋ "电脑迷" 的 "迷"

　　　　　　　➔ ＿＿＿＿＿　＿＿＿＿＿　＿＿＿＿＿
　　　　　　　　　　　new word　　*pinyin*　　English

**2.** "約好" 的 "約" ＋ "開會" 的 "會"
　　"约好" 的 "约" ＋ "开会" 的 "会"

　　　　　　　➔ ＿＿＿＿＿　＿＿＿＿＿　＿＿＿＿＿

**3.** "急忙" 的 "急" ＋ "生病" 的 "病"

　　　　　　　➔ ＿＿＿＿＿　＿＿＿＿＿　＿＿＿＿＿

**4.** "軟件" 的 "軟" ＋ "臥室" 的 "臥"
　　"软件" 的 "软" ＋ "卧室" 的 "卧"

　　　　　　　➔ ＿＿＿＿＿　＿＿＿＿＿　＿＿＿＿＿

**5.** "出版" 的 "版" ＋ "加上稅" 的 "稅"

　　　　　　　➔ ＿＿＿＿＿　＿＿＿＿＿　＿＿＿＿＿

**6.** "落伍" 的 "落" ＋ "後面" 的 "後"
　　"落伍" 的 "落" ＋ "后面" 的 "后"

　　　　　　　➔ ＿＿＿＿＿　＿＿＿＿＿　＿＿＿＿＿

**B.** Read the dialogue and answer the questions. (INTERPRETIVE)

(TRADITIONAL)

媽媽： 大明，七點了，你三點半就上網，到現在已經三個多小時了。

兒子： 七點了？糟糕，我跟小美約好七點鐘一起去聽演唱會，又要遲到了。

媽媽： 你這孩子！看你急急忙忙的樣子。七點鐘要去聽演唱會，為什麼不早點兒準備？

兒子： 我上網下載幾個軟件，一忙起來就忘了時間了。媽，我的汽車鑰匙呢？

媽媽： 鑰匙不是在你手上嗎？你老是這麼丟三拉四的，真讓我着急。每次約會都遲到，害得小美等你，她能不生氣嗎？

兒子： 沒關係，我會好好給她道歉的。再說，我下載的軟件，有一個是給她的。

媽媽： 每天老是上網下載軟件！我看你不用交女朋友了，從網上下載一個女朋友算了。

(SIMPLIFIED)

妈妈： 大明，七点了，你三点半就上网，到现在已经三个多小时了。

儿子： 七点了？糟糕，我跟小美约好七点钟一起去听演唱会，又要迟到了。

妈妈： 你这孩子！看你急急忙忙的样子。七点钟要去听演唱会，为什么不早点儿准备？

儿子： 我上网下载几个软件，一忙起来就忘了时间了。妈，我的汽车钥匙呢？

妈妈： 钥匙不是在你手上吗？你老是这么丢三拉四的，真让我着急。每次约会都迟到，害得小美等你，她能不生气吗？

儿子： 没关系，我会好好给她道歉的。再说，我下载的软件，有一个是给她的。

妈妈： 每天老是上网下载软件！我看你不用交女朋友了，从网上下载一个女朋友算了。

Questions (True/False)

( ) **1.** Daming is going to be late for the concert.

( ) **2.** Daming's mother urges her son to hurry up.

( ) **3.** When Daming uses the internet, he forgets everything else.

( ) **4.** Daming is looking for his car key while he himself has it.

( ) **5.** According to Daming's mother, Xiaomei will not wait for Daming this time.

( ) **6.** Daming is afraid that Xiaomei will break up with him.

( ) **7.** Daming's mother thinks that Daming should find a different girlfriend through the internet.

**C.** Read the passage and answer the questions. (INTERPRETIVE)

(TRADITIONAL)

現在是電腦時代，網絡對我們的生活越來越重要了。人們可以上網看新聞，查資料，玩遊戲，和朋友聊天，還可以寫博客，跟別人討論自己有興趣的問題。以前只能在圖書館查到的資料，現在可以很方便地在網上查到；以前只能在學校裏學到的東西，現在可以很方便地從網上學到。這樣下去，會不會有一天大家都覺得再也不用去圖書館，再也不用上大學了？要是世界上沒有圖書館，也沒有大學，我們的生活會怎麼樣呢？

(SIMPLIFIED)

现在是电脑时代，网络对我们的生活越来越重要了。人们可以上网看新闻，查资料，玩游戏，和朋友聊天，还可以写博客，跟别人讨论自己有兴趣的问题。以前只能在图书馆查到的资料，现在可以很方便地在网上查到；以前只能在学校里学到的东西，现在可以很方便地从网上学到。这样下去，会不会有一天大家都觉得再也不用去图书馆，再也不用上大学了？要是世界上没有图书馆，也没有大学，我们的生活会怎么样呢？

Questions (True/False)

( )　**1.**　The author is most likely a computer software advertiser.

( )　**2.**　The author believes that the internet is becoming increasingly important in people's lives.

( )　**3.**　The author is more focused on the academic use of the internet than on recreational use.

( )　**4.**　The author welcomes wholeheartedly that the internet facilitates the acquisition of information and knowledge.

( )　**5.**　The author thinks that libraries are dispensable.

**D.** Look at this newspaper ad and answer the question in English. (INTERPRETIVE)

英語口語會話保證班
外企求職應聘技巧班
兒童資優口語班
電腦商務班

英语口语会话保证班
外企求职应聘技巧班
儿童资优口语班
电脑商务班

What courses are offered? List at least two.

# IV. Writing and Grammar Exercises

## A. Building Characters

Form a character by combining the given components as indicated. Then write a word, a phrase, or a short sentence in which that character appears.

**1.** 外邊一個"門"，裏邊一個"耳"
外边一个"门"，里边一个"耳"，

是 _____ 的 _____ 。

**2.** 上邊一個"每次"的"次"，下邊一個"貝"
上边一个"每次"的"次"，下边一个"贝"，

是 _____ 的 _____ 。

3. 左邊一個人字旁，右邊一個"五"
左边一个人字旁，右边一个"五"，
是 _____ 的 _____ 。

4. 左邊一個"而且"的"且"，右邊一個"力氣"的"力"
左边一个"而且"的"且"，右边一个"力气"的"力"，
是 _____ 的 _____ 。

**B.** Let's see how addicted the main characters are to their favorite activities.

EXAMPLE:

→ 張天明玩電腦玩上癮了，甚至連上廁所的時候都上網。
張天明玩电脑玩上瘾了，甚至连上厕所的时候都上网。

1.

→ _____ 。

2.

→ _____ 。

3.

→ _____ 。

4.

→ _____ 。

**C.** Answer the questions based on the texts of the lessons.

1. 張天明的宿舍房間住得下住不下四個人？你怎麼知道？
   张天明的宿舍房间住得下住不下四个人？你怎么知道？

   →_____

   _____

2. 張天明在學校附近吃得到吃不到地道的中國菜？
   你怎麼知道？
   张天明在学校附近吃得到吃不到地道的中国菜？
   你怎么知道？

   →_____

   _____

3. 張天明離得開離不開網絡？你怎麼知道？
   张天明离得开离不开网络？你怎么知道？

   →_____

   _____

4. 麗莎受得了受不了張天明老是遲到？你怎麼知道？
   丽莎受得了受不了张天明老是迟到？你怎么知道？

   →_____

   _____

**D.** Use 結果/结果 to recap what the main characters end up doing, based on the texts of the last few lessons.

EXAMPLE:

張天明跟李哲討論選課的事，<u>結果決定選中文、經濟、和</u>
<u>電腦課</u>。

张天明跟李哲讨论选课的事，<u>结果决定选中文、经济、和</u>
<u>电脑课</u>。

**1.** 張天明去購物中心買衣服，_____。

张天明去购物中心买衣服，_____。

**2.** 柯林說這個飯館兒的雞和魚都做得不錯，

_____。

柯林说这个饭馆儿的鸡和鱼都做得不错，

_____。

**3.** 張天明知道在購物中心可以付現金，也可以用信用卡，
他没帶現金，_____。

张天明知道在购物中心可以付现金，也可以用信用卡，
他没带现金，_____。

**4.** 張天明跟大家約好了一起去看電影，

_____。

张天明跟大家约好了一起去看电影，

_____。

**E.** Fill in the blanks with either 或者 or 還是/还是.

**1. A:** 你愛吃廣東菜 _____ 湖南菜？

你爱吃广东菜 _____ 湖南菜？

**B:** 廣東菜 _____ 湖南菜，我都愛吃。

广东菜 _____ 湖南菜，我都爱吃。

**2.** 學金融專業 _____ 電腦專業對將來找工作都有幫助。

学金融专业 _____ 电脑专业对将来找工作都有帮助。

**3.** 網絡對我們的生活無論有好處 _____ 有壞處，
　我們都已經離不開網絡了。
　网络对我们的生活无论有好处 _____ 有坏处，
　我们都已经离不开网络了。

**F.** Translate the following sentences into English. (INTERPRETIVE)

**1.** 從去年十二月到今年八月，表姐都在電腦公司實習。
　从去年十二月到今年八月，表姐都在电脑公司实习。

→_____

**2.** 從高中到大學，小張都在餐館打工。
　从高中到大学，小张都在餐馆打工。

→_____

**3.** 從小到大，弟弟都不愛吃青菜。
　从小到大，弟弟都不爱吃青菜。

→_____

**4.** 這家購物中心從一層到三層都在打折。
　这家购物中心从一层到三层都在打折。

→_____

**5.** 從加州到紐約，坐飛機直飛差不多要五個多鐘頭。
　从加州到纽约，坐飞机直飞差不多要五个多钟头。

→_____

**G.** Fill in the blanks with the words or phrases given to form a coherent narrative.

(TRADITIONAL)

| | | |
|---|---|---|
| 1. 晚會 | 2. 那天晚上 | 3. 11點 |
| 4. 上個月25號 | 5. 最後 | 6. 在晚會上 |

_____，是我同屋的女朋友的生日。_____，在我們宿
舍給她開了一個小小的生日晚會。_____8點半開始。
_____，我們一邊唱歌、聊天，一邊吃東西。_____，

晚會快開完的時候，我們吃蛋糕，大家玩得很高興。

_____，我同屋的女朋友對大家說："謝謝你們！"

(SIMPLIFIED)

| | | |
|---|---|---|
| 1. 晚会 | 2. 那天晚上 | 3. 11点 |
| 4. 上个月25号 | 5. 最后 | 6. 在晚会上 |

_____，是我同屋的女朋友的生日。_____，在我们宿舍给她开了一个小小的生日晚会。_____8点半开始。

_____，我们一边唱歌、聊天，一边吃东西。_____，晚会快开完的时候，我们吃蛋糕，大家玩得很高兴。

_____，我同屋的女朋友对大家说："谢谢你们！"

**H.** Translate the following sentences into Chinese. (PRESENTATIONAL)

**1.** It's convenient to compare prices online, and shopping online is often tax free.

_____

**2.** The articles in this magazine are all garbage. Stop reading!

_____

**3.** My uncle doesn't know how to text message, send email, or surf the internet. He is so behind the times.

_____

**4.** My book is going to be formally published. Thank you for helping me with the translation.

_____

**I.** Translate the following dialogues into Chinese. (PRESENTATIONAL)

**1. A:** Hello, is this the school computing center? My computer died.

**B:** What's wrong?

**A:** Yesterday I downloaded a program. Just now I was writing an article and, at the same time, looking for references online. But I don't know why my computer just died, (which caused) the article I wrote to disappear, too.

**B:** Although the internet world is vast and very convenient, and you can find almost any reference materials, if you're careless, you can bring problems on yourself.

**A:** Then what do I do?

**B:** Please bring your computer to the school computing center. We can help you take a look.

**A:** Thank you. I'll be right there.

_____

_____

_____

_____

_____

_____

_____

_____

**2.**  Lisa:  Xuemei, Tianming spends so much time on his computer. His computer is on from morning till night.

Xuemei:  It's the age of the internet now. You cannot be without a computer.

Lisa:  When he is online, he doesn't take a break for one moment. He seems to have become addicted.

Xuemei:  Is it as serious as that?

Lisa:  He even completely forgot my birthday. In a word, I am not as important as his computer. He doesn't care about me at all.

Xuemei:  Oh, so that's what it is. No wonder you're so upset.

_____

_____

_____

_____

_____

_____

**J.** Translate the following passages into Chinese. (PRESENTATIONAL)

**1.** How convenient it is in the Age of the Internet. You can buy things, make friends, and find information online. Some people write blogs on their own websites. There are also many people who like to chat online. There is a whole other world online. The internet has made the world even bigger. Or you could say the internet has made the world even smaller. Do you agree?

_____

_____

_____

_____

_____

**2.** Do you have your own website? Do you blog? Having internet, can you do without newspapers, a telephone, or even a car? Do you often forget the time once you go online? Is your computer on from morning till night? Do you shop, order takeout, read the news, check references, and play games online? If you say "yes" to all, then you are probably addicted!

_____

_____

_____

_____

_____

**3.** Zhang Tianming's blog:
Starting tomorrow, I probably won't be able to write my blog every day because my girlfriend says I'm online all day, and she cannot take it anymore. She is going to break up with me if I don't spend more time with her. This is serious. Don't assume she is joking. She sounds like she's truly angry. I love blogging, but I love my girlfriend more.

_____

_____

_____

_____

_____

**K.** List the things you do online, and rank them based on how frequently you do them or how important they are to your daily life. (PRESENTATIONAL)

1. _____

2. _____

3. _____

4. _____

5. _____

6. _____

7. _____

**L.** Pick one thing you do online and explain why it's essential to your daily life, the impact it has on you, and why you cannot live without it. (PRESENTATIONAL)

**M.** Pick one thing you do online that you wish you could give up. Explain whether you are addicted to it, and why you want to cut down or quit. If applicable, provide alternatives to replace it. (PRESENTATIONAL)

**N.** Imagine you are going to send in a 90-second video resume to go with your job application to an international company in China. Before shooting the video, draft what you want to say about yourself. Please include basic information such as your name, background, education, skills, work experience, etc., and personal traits that are suitable for the job. (PRESENTATIONAL)

## O. Storytelling (PRESENTATIONAL)

Write a story in Chinese based on the four cartoons below. Make sure that your story has a beginning, a middle, and an end. Also make sure that the transition from one picture to the next is smooth and logical.

**1**

**2**

**3**

**4**

# I. Listening Comprehension

## A. Textbook Content (INTERPRETIVE)

Listen to the recording for the Textbook and answer the questions in English.

**1.** How do Zhang Tianming's parents pay for their son's and daughter's college education?

_____

**2.** What are the two reasons for Zhang Tianming to look for a job?

_____

**3.** How does Lisa pay for her tuition fees?

_____

**4.** Why do very few college students in China work in restaurants?

_____

**5.** How would you describe the spending habits of Lisa's roommate?

_____

## B. Workbook Dialogue (INTERPRETIVE)

Listen to the recording for the Workbook and answer the questions.

Questions (True/False):

( )  **1.**  The speakers are most likely a student and a professor.

( )  **2.**  The man has been working for about a month.

( )  **3.**  The man does not work all day on Wednesday.

( )  **4.**  By making some money, the man has reduced the burden for the woman.

Questions (Multiple Choice):

( ) **5.** How much did the man make last month?

    **a.** $100

    **b.** $400

    **c.** $500

( ) **6.** At the end of the conversation, the woman is most likely to feel _____.

    **a.** disappointed

    **b.** happy

    **c.** indifferent

## C. Workbook Narratives

**1.** Listen to the recording for the Workbook and answer the questions in English. (INTERPRETIVE)

    **a.** According to the speaker, what is the typical attitude of Chinese parents toward their children's education?

    _____

    **b.** The speaker mentions one reason for Chinese peasants to go to the cities. What is it?

    _____

    **c.** Do Chinese peasants encourage their children who are college students to look for jobs? Why or why not?

    _____

**2.** Listen to the recording for the Workbook and answer the questions in English. (INTERPRETIVE)

    **a.** Did Chinese college students have any financial pressure in the past? Why or why not?

    _____

    **b.** What is the financial situation for the parents of college students in China today?

    _____

    **c.** What difference can students make to their families' financial situation by working part time?

    _____

**3.** Listen to the recording for the Workbook and answer the questions in English. (INTERPRETIVE)

    **a.** Why do Little Bai's parents not have to pay for his tuition fees?

    _____

    **b.** How would you describe Little Bai as a son?

    _____

    **c.** What were the jobs that Little Bai has taken so far?

    _____

    **d.** How much money does Little Bai expect from his parents next month?

    _____

### D. Workbook Listening Rejoinder (INTERPERSONAL)

In this section, you will hear two people talking. After hearing the first speaker, select the best from the four possible responses given by the second speaker.

_____

## II. Speaking Exercises

**A.** Practice asking and answering the following questions. (INTERPERSONAL)

**1.** 你一邊上學一邊打工嗎？ 為什麼？
   你一边上学一边打工吗？ 为什么？

**2.** 你覺得自己的經濟壓力大不大？
   你觉得自己的经济压力大不大？

**3.** 你覺得爸爸媽媽的經濟負擔重不重？
   你觉得爸爸妈妈的经济负担重不重？

**4.** 你怎麼付學費？ 父母幫助，自己掙錢，申請獎學金，還是跟政府貸款？
   你怎么付学费？ 父母帮助，自己挣钱，申请奖学金，还是跟政府贷款？

**5.** 你一般怎麼吃飯？ 自己做，叫外賣，還是在學生餐廳吃？
   你一般怎么吃饭？ 自己做，叫外卖，还是在学生餐厅吃？

**B.** Practice speaking on the following topics. (PRESENTATIONAL)

**1.** 請談談一邊上學一邊打工對學習有什麼影響。
   请谈谈一边上学一边打工对学习有什么影响。

**2.** 請談談孩子怎麼樣可以減輕父母的經濟負擔。
   请谈谈孩子怎么样可以减轻父母的经济负担。

**3.** Imagine that you are trying to persuade your parents to allow you to work part time while in school. You need to provide good reasons to support your request and convince them that you will be both academically and financially responsible.

# III. Reading Comprehension

## A. Building Words

Complete this section by writing the characters, the *pinyin*, and the English equivalent of each new word formed. Guess the meaning before you use a dictionary to confirm.

1. "收入" 的 "入" + "門口" 的 "口"
   "收入" 的 "入" + "门口" 的 "口"

   → _____  _____  _____
              new word     *pinyin*     English

2. "身體" 的 "體" + "教育" 的 "育"
   "身体" 的 "体" + "教育" 的 "育"

   → _____  _____  _____

3. "存錢" 的 "存" + "菜單" 的 "單"
   "存钱" 的 "存" + "菜单" 的 "单"

   → _____  _____  _____

4. "管理" 的 "管" + "家庭" 的 "家"

   → _____  _____  _____

5. "零用錢" 的 "零" + "衣食住行" 的 "食"
   "零用钱" 的 "零" + "衣食住行" 的 "食"

   → _____  _____  _____

6. "工資" 的 "資" + "現金" 的 "金"
   "工资" 的 "资" + "现金" 的 "金"

   → _____  _____  _____

**B.** This is an email message sent to all students at a Chinese college by the provost's office. Read the message and answer the questions. (INTERPRETIVE)

(TRADITIONAL)

開學已經一個星期了，可是有一些同學還沒有回到學校。我們給他們的家長打電話，才知道他們在給旅行社當導遊或翻譯，還沒回來。學校覺得同學們打工，取得工作經驗，是好事。可是你們的學習比打工賺錢更重要。我們知道，你們的學費和生活費對很多父母來說壓力不小，學校也在想辦法減輕你們的經濟負擔，但是因為打工不上課是不對的。而且，如果因為打工影響了學習，應該畢業的時候不能畢業，會讓你們父母的經濟負擔更重。我們希望大家別為了打工忘了學習。

(SIMPLIFIED)

开学已经一个星期了，可是有一些同学还没有回到学校。我们给他们的家长打电话，才知道他们在给旅行社当导游或翻译，还没回来。学校觉得同学们打工，取得工作经验，是好事。可是你们的学习比打工赚钱更重要。我们知道，你们的学费和生活费对很多父母来说压力不小，学校也在想办法减轻你们的经济负担，但是因为打工不上课是不对的。而且，如果因为打工影响了学习，应该毕业的时候不能毕业，会让你们父母的经济负担更重。我们希望大家别为了打工忘了学习。

Questions (True/False)

( )  **1.**  Those students who are not back on campus yet are currently out of town.

( )  **2.**  This email sounds sympathetic to students' families' financial difficulties.

( )  **3.**  The provost's office promises to cut the tuition fees and living expenses.

( )  **4.**  According to the email, it would only make things worse for parents if a student spends too much time working.

( )  **5.**  The provost's office prohibits students from working during the semester.

**C.** Read the following email message and answer the questions. (INTERPRETIVE)

(TRADITIONAL)

爸爸：

　　您給我寄來的這個月的生活費收到了，九百塊，比上個月又多了五十塊。其實我上個月的生活費還沒用完，這個月您給我寄六百塊就夠了。在餐館工作那麼累，工資又低，您掙錢多不容易啊。每次想到這兒我就想哭。我們班有個叫毛毛的男同學，因為他爸爸有自己的公司非常有錢，就亂花錢，每天不是上飯館兒，就是唱卡拉OK，每個月他爸爸都要給他好幾千塊錢。我覺得他們心裏除了錢還是錢。我的爸爸比他們棒多了，因為您教給了我很多學校裏學不到的東西。

麗麗

(SIMPLIFIED)

爸爸：

　　您给我寄来的这个月的生活费收到了，九百块，比上个月又多了五十块。其实我上个月的生活费还没用完，这个月您给我寄六百块就够了。在餐馆工作那么累，工资又低，您挣钱多不容易啊。每次想到这儿我就想哭。我们班有个叫毛毛的男同学，因为他爸爸有自己的公司非常有钱，就乱花钱，每天不是上饭馆儿，就是唱卡拉OK，每个月他爸爸都要给他好几千块钱。我觉得他们心里除了钱还是钱。我的爸爸比他们棒多了，因为您教给了我很多学校里学不到的东西。

丽丽

Questions (True/False)

( ) **1.** Lili's monthly allowance has been increased.

( ) **2.** Lili's father owns a restaurant.

( ) **3.** Every time Lili is out of money, she will cry.

( ) **4.** Maomao covers his own expenses by working in his father's company.

( ) **5.** Lili is proud of her father because he never fails to send her money.

( ) **6.** Lili is a frugal person and considerate daughter.

**D.** Based on the employment advertisement shown here, answer the questions in English.
(INTERPRETIVE)

| | |
|---|---|
| 值班經理：1400–1700元 | 值班经理：1400–1700元 |
| 製作員：1300–1500元 | 制作员：1300–1500元 |
| 服務員：1200–1400元 | 服务员：1200–1400元 |
| 接待員：1200–1400元 | 接待员：1200–1400元 |
| 洗碗工：1200–1300元 | 洗碗工：1200–1300元 |
| 以上人員均提供食宿。 | 以上人员均提供食宿。 |
| 本店常年招聘小時工。 | 本店常年招聘小时工。 |
| 有意者請內洽值班經理。 | 有意者请内洽值班经理， |

**1.** What positions are they trying to fill? List two positions.

_____

**2.** Is there any position in the advertisement that you may be interested in applying for?
Please explain.

_____

**3.** What benefits can one get in addition to a basic salary?

_____

**E.** Based on the ad shown here, answer the questions in Chinese. (INTERPRETIVE and PRESENTATIONAL)

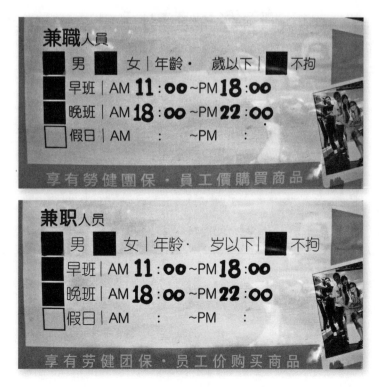

1. 請問廣告中的"早班"和"晚班"英文是什麼意思？
   请问广告中的"早班"和"晚班"英文是什么意思？

   _____

2. 你會申請這份工作嗎？為什麼？
   你会申请这份工作吗？为什么？

   _____

**F.** Look at the following form and complete the tasks. (INTERPRETIVE)

## 第一工商銀行北京市分行 繳費申請單

年　　月　　日

| 繳　費<br>種　類 | ☐ 移動話費 | ☐ 市話費 | ☐ 上網費 |
| --- | --- | --- | --- |
| | ☐ 電　費 | ☐ 收視費 | ☐ 其他 |
| 單位代碼 | | 用戶代碼 | |
| 繳費金額<br>或<br>購電度數 | | 用戶姓名 | |

為保證準確受理您的繳費業務，請協助填寫以上內容。

## 第一工商银行北京市分行 缴费申请单

年　　月　　日

| 缴　费<br>种　类 | ☐ 移动话费 | ☐ 市话费 | ☐ 上网费 |
| --- | --- | --- | --- |
| | ☐ 电　费 | ☐ 收视费 | ☐ 其他 |
| 单位代码 | | 用户代码 | |
| 缴费金额<br>或<br>购电度数 | | 用户姓名 | |

为保证准确受理您的缴费业务，请协助填写以上内容。

**1.** Circle the name of the bank.

**2.** What fees can be deducted directly from your account and paid after you fill out the form? List at least two.

_____

**3.** Sign and date the slip.

# IV. Writing and Grammar Exercises

## A. Building Characters

Form a character by combining the given components as indicated. Then write a word, a phrase, or a short sentence in which that character appears.

**1.** 左邊一個人字旁，右邊一個 "一共" 的 "共"
左边一个人字旁，右边一个 "一共" 的 "共"，
是 _____ 的 _____ 。

**2.** 左邊一個 "耳"，右邊一個 "又"
左边一个 "耳"，右边一个 "又"，
是 _____ 的 _____ 。

**3.** 上邊一個 "广"，下邊一個 "付錢" 的 "付"
上边一个 "广"，下边一个 "付钱" 的 "付"，
是 _____ 的 _____ 。

**4.** 左邊一個言字旁，右邊一個 "賣東西" 的 "賣"
左边一个言字旁，右边一个 "卖东西" 的 "卖"，
是 _____ 的 _____ 。

**B.** Draw a line connecting the verb with an object that can go with the verb.

| | |
|---|---|
| 申請/申请 | 負擔/负担 |
| 受到 | 生活 |
| 減輕/减轻 | 問題/问题 |
| 取得 | 工作 |
| 解決/解决 | 影響/影响 |
| 適應/适应 | 經驗/经验 |

**C.** Read the following conversation and fill in the blanks with the phrases provided.

(TRADITIONAL)

| 想出來 | 省下來 | 說出來 | 看出來 |
|---|---|---|---|

A: 我 _____ 你心情不好。怎麼了？有什麼事兒，_____ 聽聽。說不定我能幫忙。

B: 最近經濟不好，我父母都沒有工作。為了減輕父母的經濟負擔，我從學校宿舍搬回家住，把飯錢、住宿費都 _____，但家裏的生活費還是問題。

A: 別着急。辦法是人 _____ 的。…對了，我們出版社正好在找英文翻譯，你可以試試。

B: 是嗎？那我明天就去申請。

(SIMPLIFIED)

| 想出来 | 省下来 | 说出来 | 看出来 |
|---|---|---|---|

A: 我 _____ 你心情不好。怎么了？有什么事儿，_____ 听听。说不定我能帮忙。

B: 最近经济不好，我父母都没有工作。为了减轻父母的经济负担，我从学校宿舍搬回家住，把饭钱、住宿费都 _____，但家里的生活费还是问题。

A: 别着急。办法是人 _____ 的。…对了，我们出版社正好在找英文翻译，你可以试试。

B: 是吗？那我明天就去申请。

**D.** Fill in the blanks with either 適合/适合 or 合適/合适.

1. 小王喜歡查資料，這份研究工作對他很 _____。
   小王喜欢查资料，这份研究工作对他很 _____。

2. 你不愛跟小孩打交道，不 _____ 做家教。
   你不爱跟小孩打交道，不 _____ 做家教。

3. 他病了好幾天，我們應該去看看他。只是發短信、
打手機，我覺得不 ＿＿＿＿＿＿。

他病了好几天，我们应该去看看他。只是发短信、
打手机，我觉得不 ＿＿＿＿＿＿。

4. 這條牛仔褲長短 ＿＿＿＿＿＿，樣子、顏色也不錯，
很 ＿＿＿＿＿＿ 你。

这条牛仔裤长短 ＿＿＿＿＿＿，样子、颜色也不错，
很 ＿＿＿＿＿＿ 你。

5. 他們兩個文化背景、教育背景都不同，
在一起不 ＿＿＿＿＿＿。

他们两个文化背景、教育背景都不同，
在一起不 ＿＿＿＿＿＿。

**E.** Based on the illustrations, describe what people do.

EXAMPLE:   Teacher Li     every Saturday

→   李老師每個星期六不是洗衣服，就是打掃房間。
李老师每个星期六不是洗衣服，就是打扫房间。

**1.** Zhang Tianming's father   every night

_____

**2.**                riding the bus

_____

**3.**                when shopping for meat

_____

**F.** Connect the following individual sentences into a coherent narrative by adding connecting devices, deleting unnecessary pronouns, etc.

| | |
|---|---|
| 我去年寒假去紐約看我哥哥。 | 我去年寒假去纽约看我哥哥。 |
| 我12月16號從這裏坐飛機去紐約。 | 我12月16号从这里坐飞机去纽约。 |
| 我在飛機上坐在一個女孩兒旁邊。 | 我在飞机上坐在一个女孩儿旁边。 |
| 那個女孩很漂亮。 | 那个女孩很漂亮。 |
| 開始我不好意思跟她說話。 | 开始我不好意思跟她说话。 |
| 那個女孩要寫字。 | 那个女孩要写字, |
| 她沒帶筆。 | 她没带笔。 |
| 我很高興地把我的筆借給她。 | 我很高兴地把我的笔借给她。 |
| 她寫完字我們開始聊天。 | 她写完字我们开始聊天。 |
| 我們聊天聊得很高興。 | 我们聊天聊得很高兴。 |
| 快下飛機了，她告訴了我她的電話號碼。 | 快下飞机了，她告诉了我她的电话号码。 |
| 我說一定給她打電話。 | 我说一定给她打电话。 |

**G.** Translate the following sentences into Chinese. (PRESENTATIONAL)

**1.** I am all grown up. I should start making money to lessen my parents' financial burden.

_____

**2.** The professor suggested that we go online to read Chinese newspapers in order to improve our Chinese.

_____

**3.** On weekends, he stays in his room all day. If he's not blogging, he's playing games online.

_____

**4.** No one can stand going shopping with him. If he's not complaining about the lousy quality, he's complaining about the outrageous prices.

_____

**H.** Translate the following conversations into Chinese. (PRESENTATIONAL)

**1. A:** Why do you want to get a part-time job?

**B:** I'd like to make some spending money. If I earn the money myself, I can spend it however I want. It's liberating and I can ease my parents' burden at the same time.

**A:** Do you have time to work? Will it affect school (your studies)?

**B:** I'd like to work during summer break. It won't affect school.

**A:** Where do you want to work?

**B:** I plan to go to medical school later, so I'd like to get a job at a hospital to see if I like to deal with patients. What about you? Are you telling me that you don't want to work?

**A:** I'd like to take classes in the summer.

**B:** You can go to school and work at the same time.

_____

_____

_____

_____

_____

_____

**2. A:** Shoot, I spent too much this semester and now I have a lot of credit card debt.

**B:** Then what do you plan to do?

**A:** I haven't come up with a solution. I can only pay (it) back slowly.

**B:** Then borrow some money from your parents.

**A:** They have financial pressures, too. I would be too embarrassed to borrow money from them.

**B:** I'm doing tutoring. You can also tutor or work in computer maintenance.

**A:** I'm not suited to be a tutor, but I can maintain computers.

_____

_____

_____

_____

_____

_____

**I.** Translate the following ad into Chinese. (PRESENTATIONAL)

Do you want to make money? Do you want to gain some work experience? Do you know how to speak English? Do you know how to use a computer? Do you want to be a tutor? We are a tutoring center, and have many tutoring jobs. If you are interested, you can start applying right away. You don't need experience. We will teach you how to be a tutor, but you must like dealing with children. If you have any questions, please check out our website, or call, email, or send us a text message.

_____

_____

_____

_____

_____

_____

**J.** Translate the following email messages into Chinese. (PRESENTATIONAL)

**1.** Wenwen (文文),

Your dad and I hope that you won't work this summer. You can take some courses. If you have enough credits, you can graduate earlier and pay back the government loan earlier. If you don't want to take classes, you can relax a bit. If you need pocket money, you can borrow it from us. We know that you are a good daughter and you want to lessen our financial burden. But your sister graduated from college already, so we don't have to pay for her tuition or living expenses any more. Our burden is not as heavy as it used to be. Don't worry.

Mom

_____

_____

_____

_____

_____

_____

_____

**2.** Mom,

I don't need to borrow money from you and Dad. I've saved up some money this year. I don't owe the bank or my credit card company any money, so I don't have any financial pressure. The summer break is very long, so I can take one class and work after finishing the class. I want to work not just to make money. Gaining some work experience is also important. I will have time to have fun. Sis and I have agreed to travel to China before school starts. Her college roommate now works at a bank in Beijing. She's willing to be our tour guide. I have a Chinese test this afternoon. I have to review now. I'll call you this weekend.

Wenwen

_____

_____

_____

_____

_____

_____

_____

**K.** Suppose you are a financial advisor. Try to give students tips on how to spend and save wisely. (PRESENTATIONAL)

**a.** Compile a list of common spending problems:

_____

_____

_____

_____

**b.** Provide a list of financial dos and don'ts to help build a healthy financial future:

| Do: | Don't: |
| --- | --- |
| _____ | _____ |
| _____ | _____ |
| _____ | _____ |
| _____ | _____ |

## L. Storytelling (PRESENTATIONAL)

Write a story in Chinese based on the four cartoons below. Make sure that your story has a beginning, a middle, and an end. Also make sure that the transition from one picture to the next is smooth and logical.

**1**

**2**

**3**

**4**

9　第九課　　教育
第九课　　教育

# I. Listening Comprehension

## A. Textbook Content (INTERPRETIVE)

Listen to the recording for the Textbook and answer the questions in English.

**1.** Why do Li Zhe's brother and sister-in-law argue with each other?

_____

**2.** Why does Li Zhe's niece call Li Zhe?

_____

**3.** What kind of weekly schedule has Li Zhe's sister-in-law set up for her daughter?

_____

**4.** How would you describe Lisa's view on the issue of children's education?

_____

**5.** Why does Li You say that Li Zhe has become a "philosopher"?

_____

## B. Workbook Dialogue (INTERPRETIVE)

Listen to the recording for the Workbook and answer the questions.

Questions (True/False):

( )　**1.**　The speakers are most likely husband and wife.

( )　**2.**　Xiaoming is most likely the man's son or daughter.

( )　**3.**　Xiaoming has complained to the woman about the man.

( )　**4.**　Xiaoming enjoys his piano lessons but not his swimming lessons.

( )　**5.**　The man believes that a child must be put under some pressure in order to succeed in the future.

( )　**6.**　The man cannot become a good lawyer because he was not made to learn many things during his boyhood.

## C. Workbook Narratives

**1.** Listen to the recording for the Workbook and answer the questions in English. (INTERPRETIVE)

**a.** How did Little Qian feel when he first landed the new job? Why?

_____

**b.** When did things change for Little Qian?

_____

**c.** What kinds of phone calls did Little Qian receive?

_____

**d.** How would you describe Little Qian's reaction to those phone calls?

_____

**2.** Listen to the recording for the Workbook and answer the questions in English. (INTERPRETIVE)

**a.** What are Anthony's parents interested in, respectively?

_____

**b.** Do Anthony's parents agree on what their son should learn?

_____

**c.** Does Anthony share either of his parents' interests?

_____

**3.** Listen to the recording for the Workbook and answer the questions in English. (INTERPRETIVE)

**a.** Who is the speaker?

_____

**b.** Whom is the speaker addressing?

_____

**c.** According to the speaker, what problem do the children have?

_____

**d.** How would you describe the speaker's view on the issue of children's education?

_____

## D. Workbook Listening Rejoinder (INTERPERSONAL)

In this section, you will hear two people talking. After hearing the first speaker, select the best from the four possible responses given by the second speaker.

---

# II. Speaking Exercises

**A.** Practice asking and answering the following questions. (INTERPERSONAL)

**1.** 你小時候學過鋼琴、畫畫兒、外語嗎？

你小时候学过钢琴、画画儿、外语吗？

**2.** 如果學過，學了多長時間？是你自己想學的？還是父母要你學的？

如果学过，学了多长时间？是你自己想学的？还是父母要你学的？

**3.** 你童年的時候學習壓力大不大？有沒有時間玩？

你童年的时候学习压力大不大？有没有时间玩？

**B.** Practice speaking on the following topics. (INTERPERSONAL)

**1.** 如果你的學習壓力很大，你怎麼讓自己輕鬆一些？

如果你的学习压力很大，你怎么让自己轻松一些？

**2.** 你理解父母下課以後或週末送孩子學這學那的做法嗎？你同意嗎？為什麼？

你理解父母下课以后或周末送孩子学这学那的做法吗？你同意吗？为什么？

**3.** Suppose you could relive your childhood. Express what you wish your parents and/or you had done differently in terms of your schoolwork and extracurricular activities.

# III. Reading Comprehension

## A. Building Words

Complete this section by writing the characters, the pinyin, and the English equivalent of each new word formed. Guess the meaning before you use a dictionary to confirm.

**1.** "美滿"的"滿" + "意見"的"意"
"美满"的"满" + "意见"的"意"

→ _____  _____  _____
　　　　　　　new word　　*pinyin*　　English

**2.** "抱怨"的"怨" + "生氣"的"氣"
"抱怨"的"怨" + "生气"的"气"

→ _____  _____  _____

**3.** "學校"的"校" + "家長"的"長"
"学校"的"校" + "家长"的"长"

→ _____  _____  _____

**4.** "口水"的"口" + "鋼琴"的"琴"
"口水"的"口" + "钢琴"的"琴"

→ _____  _____  _____

**5.** "農村"的"農" + "事業"的"業"
"农村"的"农" + "事业"的"业"

→ _____  _____  _____

**B.** Read the conversation and answer the questions. (INTERPRETIVE)

(TRADITIONAL)

柯林：雪梅，你鋼琴彈得棒極了！你是幾歲開始學的鋼琴？

雪梅：四歲。

柯林：你怎麼四歲就開始對鋼琴有興趣了？

雪梅：哈，我四歲的時候沒見過幾次鋼琴，怎麼會有興趣？我
　　　媽媽開始帶我上鋼琴學校的時候，我一看見鋼琴就哭。
　　　可是媽媽一定要上完課才帶我回家。

柯林：她怎麼能讓你學你沒有興趣的東西呢?

雪梅：我媽媽有她的道理。她說，學鋼琴要早，等到孩子自己對鋼琴有興趣，可能就太晚了。

柯林：有道理。我十歲的時候開始喜歡鋼琴，後來也學了好幾年，可是現在跟你比，差得太多了。

雪梅：我的愛好和興趣是媽媽幫我選擇的。一開始我常常抱怨，可是後來我就真的喜歡鋼琴了，越學越輕鬆，越學越快樂。

柯林：現在我開始理解像你媽媽那樣的父母教育孩子的做法了。

(SIMPLIFIED)

柯林：雪梅，你钢琴弹得棒极了！你是几岁开始学的钢琴?

雪梅：四岁。

柯林：你怎么四岁就开始对钢琴有兴趣了?

雪梅：哈，我四岁的时候没见过几次钢琴，怎么会有兴趣? 我妈妈开始带我上钢琴学校的时候，我一看见钢琴就哭。可是妈妈一定要上完课才带我回家。

柯林：她怎么能让你学你没有兴趣的东西呢?

雪梅：我妈妈有她的道理。她说，学钢琴要早，等到孩子自己对钢琴有兴趣，可能就太晚了。

柯林：有道理。我十岁的时候开始喜欢钢琴，后来也学了好几年，可是现在跟你比，差得太多了。

雪梅：我的爱好和兴趣是妈妈帮我选择的。一开始我常常抱怨，可是后来我就真的喜欢钢琴了，越学越轻松，越学越快乐。

柯林：现在我开始理解像你妈妈那样的父母教育孩子的做法了。

Questions (True/False):

( ) **1.** When Xuemei started taking piano lessons, she was not interested in them.

( ) **2.** Xuemei often cried when her mother took her away from the piano school.

( ) **3.** Xuemei's mother insisted that a child should start taking piano lessons early.

( ) **4.** Ke Lin's parents made him take piano lessons when he was ten.

( ) **5.** According to Ke Lin, Xuemei plays piano better than he does.

( ) **6.** Xuemei sounds quite grateful that her mother forced her to take piano lessons when she was young.

( ) **7.** Ke Lin has always been sympathetic to Xuemei's mother's ideas about children's education.

**C.** Read the passage and answer the questions. (INTERPRETIVE)

(TRADITIONAL)

在中國，很多父母都希望自己的孩子學的東西越多越好，這樣孩子長大了才能做出一番大事業。因為有這種望子成龍望女成鳳的想法，所以很多家長把孩子的課外時間安排得滿滿的，學了這個又去學那個，不太考慮孩子自己的興趣和愛好。很多孩子因為太忙，休息不夠，影響了身體健康。還有不少孩子因為壓力太大，沒有時間跟其他小朋友一起玩兒，所以覺得自己的童年不快樂。北京有個十二歲的男孩兒說："爸爸媽媽一直希望我長大了成為一條龍。可是當一條不快樂的龍，不如當一條快樂的蟲。"    （蟲： chóng, insect; bug）

(SIMPLIFIED)

在中国，很多父母都希望自己的孩子学的东西越多越好，这样孩子长大了才能做出一番大事业。因为有这种望子成龙望女成凤的想法，所以很多家长把孩子的课外时间安排得满满的，学了这个又去学那个，不太考虑孩子自己的兴趣和爱好。很多孩子因为太忙，休息不够，影响了身体健康。还有不少孩子因为压力太大，没有时间跟其它小朋友一起玩儿，所以觉得自己的童年不快乐。北京有个十二岁的男孩儿说："爸爸妈妈一直希望我长大了成为一条龙。可是当一条不快乐的龙，不如当一条快乐的虫。"    （虫： chóng, insect; bug）

Questions (True/False):

( )　**1.** The author asserts that many Chinese parents place very high expectations on their children.

( )　**2.** Some Chinese children are too busy because they are interested in too many things.

( )　**3.** The author believes that being too busy could be detrimental to children's health.

( )　**4.** Some children have to be pressured to spend some time playing with their friends.

( )　**5.** The twelve-year-old boy fully understands his parents' efforts to make him study harder.

( )　**6.** The author disapproves of the practice of forcing children to learn many things.

**D.** Look at this newspaper ad and answer the following questions in English. (INTERPRETIVE)

**1.** What classes can parents sign their children up for? List at least four.

_____

**2.** Is the ad targeting students in grade school, junior high, or senior high? How do you know?

_____

**3.** Circle the words that mean "tutorial services."

_____

**E.** Look at this newspaper ad and answer the following questions in English. (INTERPRETIVE)

小初高教師1對1
暑假輕鬆自在提成績，上學大教育！
一綫教師1對1面授
授課陪讀答疑3種教學模式
知識 習慣 方法 3方面提高

小初高 教师1对1
暑假轻松自在提成绩，上学大教育！
一线教师1对1面授
授课陪读答疑3种教学模式
知识 习惯 方法 3方面提高

**1.** What's the teacher–student ratio?

_____

**2.** What time of year does this ad encourage people to sign up for classes?

_____

**3.** In which areas does the ad guarantee good results? Name at least one.

_____

# IV. Writing and Grammar Exercises

## A. Building Characters

Form a character by combining the given components as indicated. Then write a word, a phrase, or a short sentence in which that character appears.

**1.** 左邊一個人字旁，右邊一個 "至於" 的 "至"
左边一个人字旁，右边一个 "至于" 的 "至"，
是 _____ 的 _____ 。

**2.** 左邊一個提手旁，右邊一個 "非常" 的 "非"
左边一个提手旁，右边一个 "非常" 的 "非"，
是 _____ 的 _____ 。

**3.** 上邊兩個 "王"，下邊一個 "今天" 的 "今"
上边两个 "王"，下边一个 "今天" 的 "今"，
是 _____ 的 _____ 。

**4.** 左邊一個 "木"，右邊一個 "剛才" 的 "才"
左边一个 "木"，右边一个 "刚才" 的 "才"，
是 _____ 的 _____ 。

**B.** Fill in the blanks with 的, 得, or 地.

(TRADITIONAL)

我們兩個相處_____那麼好，我理解你_____想法，你同意我_____看法，我一直以為你是我_____知音。可是没想到為了借錢，我們吵架吵_____那麼厲害。到底什麼重要？錢還是朋友？我們應該好好兒_____想想。

(SIMPLIFIED)

我们两个相处_____那么好，我理解你_____想法，你同意我_____看法，我一直以为你是我_____知音。可是没想到为了借钱，我们吵架吵_____那么厉害。到底什么重要？钱还是朋友？我们应该好好儿_____想想。

**C.** Reply to the following statements to set the record straight.

EXAMPLE:

**A:** 林雪梅是從上海來的吧？
　　林雪梅是从上海来的吧？

**B:** <u>林雪梅不是從上海來的</u>，<u>而是從杭州來的</u>。
　　<u>林雪梅不是从上海来的</u>，<u>而是从杭州来的</u>。

**1. A:** 聽說林雪梅愛吃辣的？
　　听说林雪梅爱吃辣的？

**B:** _____ 。

**2. A:** 張天明下個學期好像選了金融課。
　　张天明下个学期好像选了金融课。

**B:** _____ 。

**3. A:** 麗莎對球賽很有興趣吧？
　　丽莎对球赛很有兴趣吧？

**B:** _____ 。

**4. A:** 聽説麗莎不准張天明上網?

　　听说丽莎不准张天明上网?

　　**B:** _____ 。

**5. A:** 麗莎好像同意李哲嫂子的做法。

　　丽莎好像同意李哲嫂子的做法。

　　**B:** _____ 。

**D.** Practice asking and answering questions based on the following topics.

EXAMPLE:

　　children　　　studying vs. having fun　　　important

→　Question: <u>你認為孩子學習重要還是玩兒重要?</u>
　　　　　　<u>你认为孩子学习重要还是玩儿重要?</u>
　　Answer:　<u>我認為孩子(your choice)重要</u> 。
　　　　　　<u>我认为孩子(your choice)重要</u> 。

**1.**　Li Zhe　　　finding a job vs. going to graduate school　　　good

→　**Q:** _____ 。

　　**A:** _____ 。

**2.**　Zhang Tianming　　living on campus vs. living off campus　　good

→　**Q:** _____ 。

　　**A:** _____ 。

**3.**　Zhang Tianming　studying literature vs. studying finance　appropriate

→　**Q:** _____ 。

　　**A:** _____ 。

**4.**　Lin Xuemei　　studying vs. dating　　important

→　**Q:** _____ 。

　　**A:** _____ 。

**E.** Fill in the blanks with the words and phrases given to form a coherent narrative.

(TRADITIONAL)

> 1. 結果　2. 我　3. 雖然　4. 可是　5. 可是
> 6. 於是　7. 後來　8. 今天早上　9. 昨天　10. 在購物中心

_____我在網上看見學校附近的購物中心很多商店在打折。_____起床後我就開車去那個購物中心。_____，很多商店真的都打折，我很高興。_____想買一套運動服，_____走進了一家賣運動服的商店。進去一看，什麼都打6折，我覺得不錯。_____我一看價錢，_____是打6折，_____還得好幾百塊。_____我又去了幾家商店，_____，什麼都沒買，就回家了。

(SIMPLIFIED)

> 1. 结果　2. 我　3. 虽然　4. 可是　5. 可是
> 6. 于是　7. 后来　8. 今天早上　9. 昨天　10. 在购物中心

_____我在网上看见学校附近的购物中心很多商店在打折。_____起床后我就开车去那个购物中心。_____，很多商店真的都打折，我很高兴。_____想买一套运动服，_____走进了一家卖运动服的商店。进去一看，什么都打6折，我觉得不错。_____我一看价钱，_____是打6折，_____还得好几百块。_____我又去了几家商店，_____，什么都没买，就回家了。

**F.** Translate the following sentences into Chinese. (PRESENTATIONAL)

**1.** He was crying nonstop, like a little kid.

_____

**2.** It took her a lot of effort to get her master's degree.

_____

**G.** Translate the following dialogues into Chinese using 而. (PRESENTATIONAL)

**1. A:** Is your major history?

   **B:** My major is not history, but economics.

_____

_____

**2. A:** Are you a computer science Ph.D.?

   **B:** I'm not a computer science Ph.D., but a chemistry Ph.D.

_____

_____

**3. A:** Mom, are you against my marrying Little Wang?

   **B:** I am not against it, but think it's too early for you to get married now. You'd better graduate from college before getting married.

_____

_____

_____

**4. A:** I haven't seen your boyfriend Little Lin for a while. Did you two have a falling out?

   **B:** Contrary to what you think, we didn't have a fight. He went to Mexico to study abroad and won't be back until next winter.

   **A:** So that means you broke up?

   **B:** Actually, we didn't break up. We chat online every single day.

_____

_____

_____

_____

_____

**5. A:** Little Zhang, where did you say you'll have to take your son on Friday evening?

**B:** I'll have to take him to learn swimming. Saturday I'll have to take him to a skating lesson.

**A:** I hope you get a day's rest on Sunday.

**B:** No, on Sunday I'll have to take my son to a piano lesson.

**A:** Your son is still just a kid. Won't he complain?

**B:** No, he loves learning these things. One moment he's learning this, and the other moment he's learning that. When we see how happy he is learning, we are happy, too.

_____

_____

_____

_____

**6. A:** Little Gao, your older brother and sister-in-law are both teachers. Their opinions wouldn't differ in terms of education, right?

**B:** Not necessarily. Although they are both teachers, their opinions often do differ when it comes to their child's education. My sister-in-law thinks that children should play, but my brother packs their child's schedule and wants him to take this lesson or take that lesson.

**A:** Whose opinion do you agree with?

**B:** I think both their views make sense. I think that when children play they also learn. Is children's playing learning? It depends on what you think is learning: many things you learn from life, and of course you can also acquire a lot of knowledge from books and at school. I think my sister-in-law would definitely agree, because she is a teacher herself. But their child is only eight. He ought to play more.

**A:** So one could say that you actually agree with your sister-in-law!

_____

_____

_____

_____

_____

_____

**H.** Translate the following passages into Chinese. (PRESENTATIONAL)

**1.** Many Chinese parents want their sons and daughters to become distinguished and successful like dragons and phoenixes. They hope that their children will be good students when they are young and will have successful careers later, so they give their children a lot of pressure. However, Bai Xiaolin's (白小林) parents only hope that he will have a happy life. I don't think this is because they feel that Bai Xiaolin is incapable of being a good student or that he is incapable of having a great career in the future. On the contrary, this is because they feel that the most important thing in life is to be happy. As a matter of fact, Bai Xiaolin is a very good student. He will become an accomplished person.

_____

_____

_____

_____

_____

_____

**2.** The Chinese used to think that men must be accomplished and women must be beautiful. Li Zhe's sister-in-law considers this kind of thinking very outdated. Nowadays there are many women with master's degrees and Ph.Ds, who design and manage websites or are college professors. And why is it that men don't need to be good-looking? Li Zhe's older brother said it would be best for everyone to be as intelligent and good-looking as Li Zhe's sister-in-law. Li Zhe's sister-in-law said that his brother was being too "glib."

_____

_____

_____

_____

_____

_____

**3.** Do you want your sons and daughters to become distinguished and successful like dragons and phoenixes? Do you want your children to have great careers? If you do, our college student tutors can make your children become the accomplished people that society needs! Our tutors can teach English, computer science, chemistry, piano, Chinese...Do not wait a moment longer. Hurry! Call us immediately!

_____

_____

_____

_____

_____

**I.** Design an after-school or weekend program in Chinese that will, on the one hand, satisfy parents' desire to help their children live up to their full potential, and on the other hand, be enjoyable for the children. (PRESENTATIONAL)

**J.** Prepare a sales pitch to promote the program that you have designed in Exercise I. Make sure to entice both parents and their children by offering a variety of classes, reasonable fees, and flexible hours, and show that you can guarantee good results while letting children have fun at the same time. (PRESENTATIONAL)

## K. Storytelling (PRESENTATIONAL)

Write a story in Chinese based on the four cartoons below. Make sure that your story has a beginning, a middle, and an end. Also make sure that the transition from one picture to the next is smooth and logical.

**1**

**2**

**3**

**4**

第十課　中國地理
第十课　中国地理

# I. Listening Comprehension

## A. Textbook Content (INTERPRETIVE)

Listen to the recording for the Textbook and answer the questions in English.

**1.** Why are Zhang Tianming and Lisa studying a map of China?

_____

**2.** Which Chinese city does Zhang Tianming suggest that they visit first? Why?

_____

**3.** According to Zhang Tianming, why is it not a good time to visit Harbin?

_____

**4.** Why do most of the rivers in China flow eastward?

_____

**5.** What geographical similarities do they see between China and the United States?

_____

**6.** Why do they finally decide to go to Yunnan?

_____

## B. Workbook Dialogue (INTERPRETIVE)

Listen to the recording for the Workbook and answer the questions.

Questions (True/False):

( )　**1.** The speakers are planning their trip to Yunnan.

( )　**2.** According to the man, the weather in northern Yunnan is balmy all year round.

( )　**3.** Based on the conversation, the natural conditions in Yunnan are diverse.

( )　**4.** This conversation most likely takes place in October.

( )　**5.** According to the man, there are only two seasons in southern Yunnan.

( )　**6.** The man learned about the climate in Yunnan in his geography class.

## C. Workbook Narratives

1. Listen to the recording for the Workbook and answer the questions in English. (INTERPRETIVE)

   **a.** Who is the speaker, and to whom is he speaking?

   _____

   **b.** What kind of place are they going to visit?

   _____

   **c.** What is the arrangement for lunch?

   _____

2. Listen to the recording for the Workbook and answer the questions in English. (INTERPRETIVE)

   **a.** Is the speaker familiar with the person she is speaking to? How do you know?

   _____

   **b.** What is the difference between visiting Harbin in summer and visiting Harbin in winter?

   _____

   **c.** What is the speaker's advice to the other person?

   _____

3. Listen to the recording for the Workbook and answer the questions in English. (INTERPRETIVE)

   **a.** Is the speaker now in the United States? When was the last time he talked to Wang Laoshi?

   _____

   **b.** Who is more familiar with the United States, the speaker or Wang Laoshi?

   _____

   **c.** What advice did Wang Laoshi give to the speaker? How does the speaker like it?

   _____

   **d.** Is New York likely to be on the speaker's itinerary next time he visits the United States? Why or why not?

   _____

### D. Workbook Listening Rejoinder (INTERPERSONAL)

In this section, you will hear two people talking. After hearing the first speaker, select the best from the four possible responses given by the second speaker.

---

## II. Speaking Exercises

**A.** Practice asking and answering the following questions. (INTERPERSONAL)

國家/国家 (guójiā): country

1. 你的家鄉在你的國家的東部、西部、南部、北部還是中部？

   你的家乡在你的国家的东部、西部、南部、北部还是中部？

2. 北京是中國的首都和文化中心，上海是中國的經濟中心。你的國家的首都是哪一個城市？你的國家的文化中心是哪一個城市？你的國家的經濟中心是哪一個城市？

   北京是中国的首都和文化中心，上海是中国的经济中心。你的国家的首都是哪一个城市？你的国家的文化中心是哪一个城市？你的国家的经济中心是哪一个城市？

3. 你的國家有高山嗎？如果有，大多在東部、南部、西部還是北部？

   你的国家有高山吗？如果有，大多在东部、南部、西部还是北部？

4. 你的國家最長的河流是什麼河？從哪邊往哪邊流？

   你的国家最长的河流是什么河？从哪边往哪边流？

5. 你的國家有沙漠嗎？在東部、南部、西部還是北部？

   你的国家有沙漠吗？在东部、南部、西部还是北部？

**B.** Practice speaking on the following topics. (PRESENTATIONAL)

1. 請簡單介紹一下中國地理。

   请简单介绍一下中国地理。

**2.** 請比較你的國家和中國的地形、緯度、面積、人口。

請比較你的国家和中国的地形、纬度、面积、人口。

**3.** If you have been to China, describe the city/province/region that impresses you the most, including its topography, climate, natural scenery, people, and food. If you have never been to China, name the city/province/region that you would most like to visit, and explain why you have chosen that place.

# III. Reading Comprehension

## A. Building Words

Complete this section by writing the characters, the *pinyin*, and the English equivalent of each new word formed. Guess the meaning before you use a dictionary to confirm.

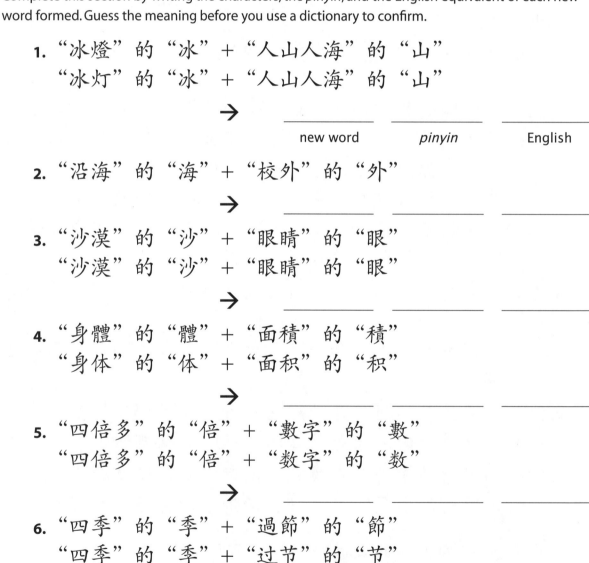

**1.** "冰燈" 的 "冰" + "人山人海" 的 "山"

"冰灯" 的 "冰" + "人山人海" 的 "山"

→ _____ _____ _____

                                 new word     *pinyin*     English

**2.** "沿海" 的 "海" + "校外" 的 "外"

→ _____ _____ _____

**3.** "沙漠" 的 "沙" + "眼睛" 的 "眼"

"沙漠" 的 "沙" + "眼睛" 的 "眼"

→ _____ _____ _____

**4.** "身體" 的 "體" + "面積" 的 "積"

"身体" 的 "体" + "面积" 的 "积"

→ _____ _____ _____

**5.** "四倍多" 的 "倍" + "數字" 的 "數"

"四倍多" 的 "倍" + "数字" 的 "数"

→ _____ _____ _____

**6.** "四季" 的 "季" + "過節" 的 "節"

"四季" 的 "季" + "过节" 的 "节"

→ _____ _____ _____

**B.** Read the passage and answer the questions. (INTERPRETIVE)

(TRADITIONAL)

中國人口多，喜歡旅遊的人也越來越多。過節或者放假的時候，有名的旅遊景點都是人山人海，擠得很。其實去中國旅遊，並不一定非去那幾個最有名的地方不可。中國那麼大，漂亮的地方和有意思的地方多極了。雲南的西南部就有一個很特別的地方，那兒有好幾個少數民族，我們上次去那兒，他們都非常客氣。那兒的自然風景特別美，天氣也好，知道的人不多，所以一點兒也不擠。下次你去雲南，一定要去那兒看看。那兒雖然離飛機場非常遠，可是坐火車和汽車很方便。

(SIMPLIFIED)

中国人口多，喜欢旅游的人也越来越多。过节或者放假的时候，有名的旅游景点都是人山人海，挤得很。其实去中国旅游，并不一定非去那几个最有名的地方不可。中国那么大，漂亮的地方和有意思的地方多极了。云南的西南部就有一个很特别的地方，那儿有好几个少数民族，我们上次去那儿，他们都非常客气。那儿的自然风景特别美，天气也好，知道的人不多，所以一点儿也不挤。下次你去云南，一定要去那儿看看。那儿虽然离飞机场非常远，可是坐火车和汽车很方便。

Questions (True/False):

( ) **1.** The author wants to visit Yunnan because he has never been there.

( ) **2.** The author suggests that the more frequently visited tourist attractions are more beautiful.

( ) **3.** The passage mentions a place that is becoming a major tourist attraction.

( ) **4.** That place in Yunnan has beautiful scenery and nice weather.

( ) **5.** That place is easily accessible by train, but not by airplane.

**C.** Read the passage and answer the questions. (INTERPRETIVE)

(TRADITIONAL)

　　藍天旅遊公司歡迎您參加我們的旅遊計畫。很多人都覺得過中國新年應該回家，待在家裏。其實，新年我們有一個多星期的假，是最好的旅遊時間，為什麼非在家裏過年不可呢？我們這裏冬天自然條件不太好，非常冷，為什麼不去南邊走走？為什麼不去看看廣州和深圳，去看看大海，或者去看看四季如春的雲南？大家不用擔心飛機票太貴，因為航空公司會給我們打七折。如果您對去中國南部旅遊有興趣，請趕快給我們打電話。我們一定會給您和您的家人安排一個非常特別的新年假期。

(SIMPLIFIED)

　　蓝天旅游公司欢迎您参加我们的旅游计划。很多人都觉得过中国新年应该回家，待在家里。其实，新年我们有一个多星期的假，是最好的旅游时间，为什么非在家里过年不可呢？我们这里冬天自然条件不太好，非常冷，为什么不去南边走走？为什么不去看看广州和深圳，去看看大海，或者去看看四季如春的云南？大家不用担心飞机票太贵，因为航空公司会给我们打七折。如果您对去中国南部旅游有兴趣，请赶快给我们打电话。我们一定会给您和您的家人安排一个非常特别的新年假期。

Questions (True/False):

(　　) **1.** This message is from a tourist agency.

(　　) **2.** The intended readers of this message are residents of Guangzhou and Shenzhen.

(　　) **3.** According to the message, those who sign up will get airplane tickets at favorable prices.

(　　) **4.** Weather conditions at the destinations mentioned are a major selling point of this message.

(　　) **5.** Interested people should go online to sign up.

**D.** Look at the following weather forecast and answer the question. (INTERPRETIVE)

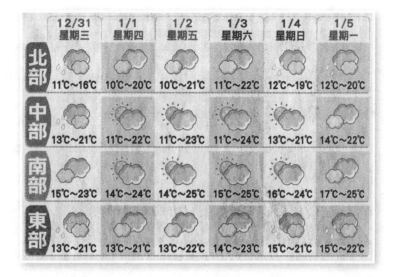

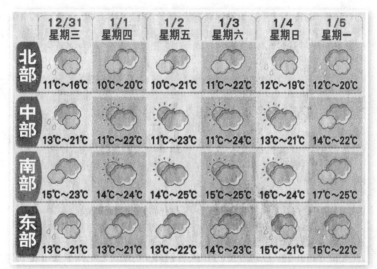

On average, which region has the coldest weather?

_____

**E.** Look at the following newspaper ad and answer the questions. (INTERPRETIVE)

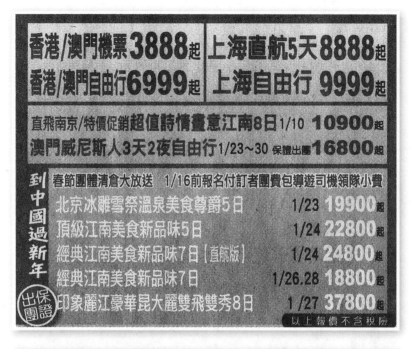

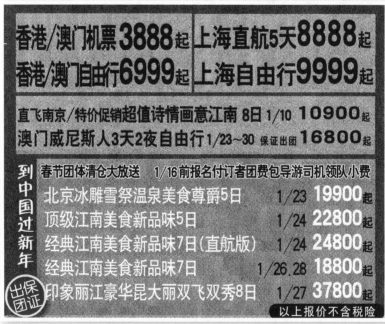

**1.** What destination cities does it offer? List at least four.

_____

**2.** What time of year will these tours depart?

_____

**3.** What do 直航 and 自由行 mean?

_____

**F.** Look at the following newspaper ad and answer the questions. (INTERPRETIVE)

雲南
四星純玩－昆明.大理.麗江雙飛雙汽6日麗江含小索道　3060
昆明.大理.麗江.瀘沽湖/香格里拉　　　　　　雙飛雙臥8日　2510起
昆明.大理.麗江.版納(野象谷)　三飛一臥7/四飛一臥8日　3230起
昆明.大理.麗江.中甸豪華品質團　四星+五星　雙飛雙汽8日　3380
昆明.大理.麗江.虎跳峽豪華純玩團　四星+五星　三飛6日　4030

西藏
拉薩.布達拉宮.大昭寺.羊八井.納木錯.羊湖.日喀則.扎什倫布寺
　　　　　　　　　　　　　　　雙臥10/單飛8日　2540起
拉薩.布達拉宮.大昭寺.羊八井.納木錯.林芝.巴松錯湖.巨柏林
　　　　　　　　　　　　　　　雙臥10/單飛8日　2590起
西寧.青海湖+西藏　　　　　　雙飛一臥8/10日　4750起

海南
四星純玩(含蜈支洲或南山)　　　　　　　　雙飛5日　2100起
海洋任我遊2日行程+2日自由　三亞往返　五星住宿　雙飛5日　2350
三亞4晚5天自由人(機票+自選3-5星酒店　單訂特價機票)2300起

桂林
南寧.越南(下龍.河內)+北海三星品質團雙臥9/雙飛6日　2380起
南寧+德天瀑布+通靈+北海三星品質團雙臥7/雙飛5日　1900起

新疆
烏魯木齊.土魯番.葡萄溝.天山天池.敦煌.月牙泉.嘉峪關.蘭州
　　　　　　　　　　　　　　　　　雙飛6日　3500
烏魯木齊.土魯番.葡萄溝.天山天池.魔鬼城.布爾津.喀納斯
　　　　　　　　　　　　　　　　　雙飛7日　3750

云南
四星纯玩－昆明.大理.丽江双飞双汽6日丽江含小索道　3060
昆明.大理.丽江.泸沽湖/香格里拉　　　　　　双飞双卧8日　2510起
昆明.大理.丽江.版纳(野象谷)　三飞一卧7/四飞一卧8日　3230起
昆明.大理.丽江.中甸豪华品质团　四星+五星　双飞双汽8日　3380
昆明.大理.丽江.虎跳峡豪华纯玩团　四星+五星　三飞6日　4030

西藏
拉萨.布达拉宫.大昭寺.羊八井.纳木错.羊湖.日喀则.扎什伦布寺
　　　　　　　　　　　　　　　双卧10/单飞8日　2540起
拉萨.布达拉宫.大昭寺.羊八井.纳木错.林芝.巴松错湖.巨柏林
　　　　　　　　　　　　　　　双卧10/单飞8日　2590起
西宁.青海湖+西藏　　　　　　双飞一卧8/10日　4750起

海南
四星纯玩(含蜈支洲或南山)　　　　　　　　双飞5日　2100起
海洋任我游2日行程+2日自由　三亚往返　五星住宿　双飞5日　2350
三亚4晚5天自由人(机票+自选3-5星酒店 单订特价机票)2300起

桂林
南宁.越南(下龙.河内)+北海三星品质团双卧9/双飞6日　2380起
南宁+德天瀑布+通灵+北海银滩三星品质团双卧7/双飞5日　1900起

新疆
乌鲁木齐.土鲁番.葡萄沟.天山天池.敦煌.月牙泉.嘉峪关.兰州
　　　　　　　　　　　　　　　　双飞6日　3500
乌鲁木齐.土鲁番.葡萄沟.天山天池.魔鬼城.布尔津.喀纳斯
　　　　　　　　　　　　　　　　双飞7日　3750

**1.** How many tours are heading to Yunnan? _____

**2.** Among the Yunnan tours, which one would you prefer? Why?

_____

**3.** What do 飛/飞, 汽, and 五星 refer to in English?

_____

# IV. Writing and Grammar Exercises

## A. Building Characters

Form a character by combining the given components as indicated. Then write a word, a phrase, or a short sentence in which that character appears.

**1.** 左邊一個三點水，右邊一個 "可能" 的 "可"
左边一个三点水，右边一个 "可能" 的 "可" ，
是 _____ 的 _____ 。

**2.** 上邊一個 "佳" ，下邊一個 "木"
上边一个 "佳" ，下边一个 "木" ，
是 _____ 的 _____ 。

**3.** 左邊一個三點水，右邊一個 "打工" 的 "工"
左边一个三点水，右边一个 "打工" 的 "工" ，
是 _____ 的 _____ 。

**4.** 左邊一個 "土" ，右邊一個 "四川" 的 "川"
左边一个 "土" ，右边一个 "四川" 的 "川" ，
是 _____ 的 _____ 。

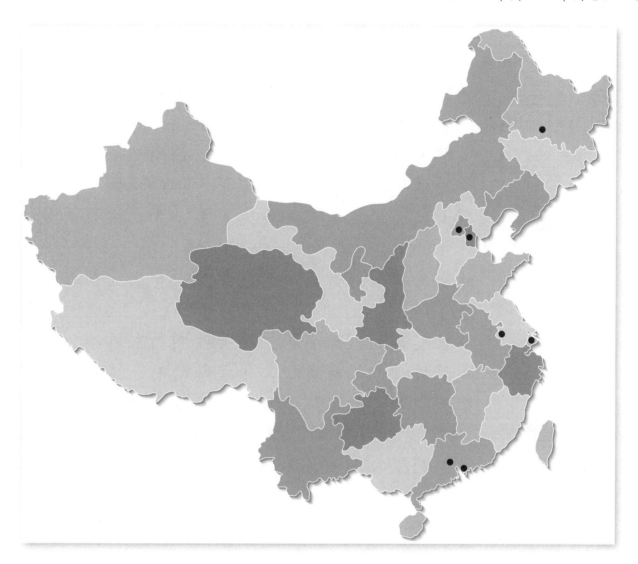

**B.** Locate the following cities on the map by placing the corresponding numbers next to their locations.

| | | | |
|---|---|---|---|
| **1.** 廣州／广州 | **2.** 哈爾濱／哈尔滨 | **3.** 南京 | **4.** 北京 |
| **5.** 天津 | **6.** 上海 | **7.** 深圳 | |

**C.** Fill in the blanks with either 因為／因为 or 為了／为了.

1. _____研究中國的少數民族，王教授在雲南待了一年
半。

_____研究中国的少数民族，王教授在云南待了一年
半。

2. _____ 新年假期旅遊景點人太多，小李決定不出門，在家休息。

_____ 新年假期旅游景点人太多，小李决定不出门，在家休息。

3. _____ 了解世界地理，張先生買了一張新地圖。

_____ 了解世界地理，张先生买了一张新地图。

4. _____ 讓女兒將來能做出一番大事業，李太太讓女兒從小就學這學那。

_____ 让女儿将来能做出一番大事业，李太太让女儿从小就学这学那。

5. _____ 減輕父母的經濟負擔，張天明想打工掙錢。

_____ 减轻父母的经济负担，张天明想打工挣钱。

6. _____ 張天明整天離不開電腦，大家覺得他玩電腦玩上癮了。

_____ 张天明整天离不开电脑，大家觉得他玩电脑玩上瘾了。

**D.** Give an account of what the IC characters like to do based on the visual clues. Use 而 in your answers.

EXAMPLE:

→ 柯林喜歡發電郵聊天兒，而林雪梅喜歡打電話聊天兒。
柯林喜欢发电邮聊天儿，而林雪梅喜欢打电话聊天儿。

1.

→ _____ 。

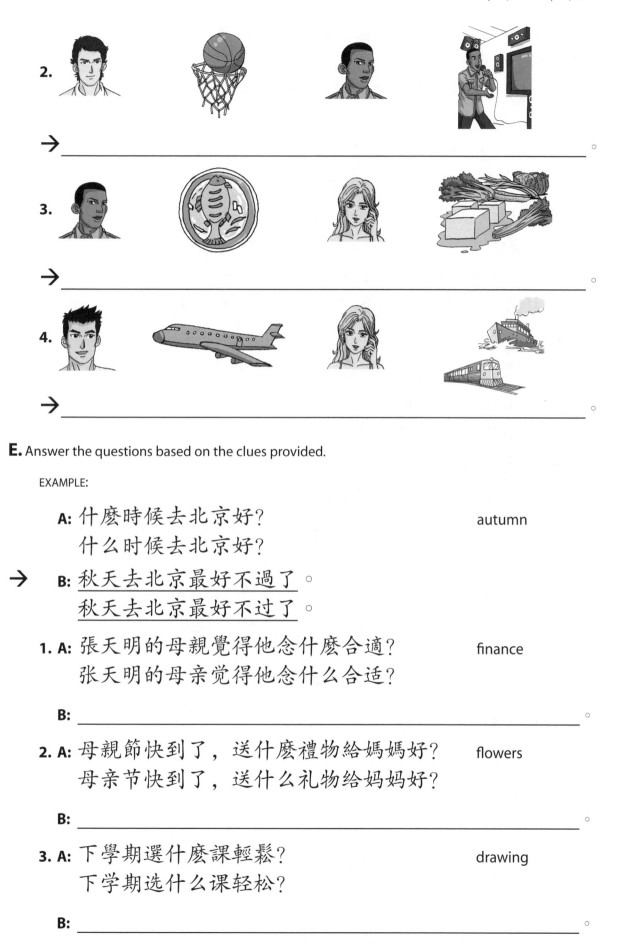

**2.**

→ _____ 。

**3.**

→ _____ 。

**4.**

→ _____ 。

**E.** Answer the questions based on the clues provided.

EXAMPLE:

**A:** 什麼時候去北京好?　　　　　　　　autumn
什么时候去北京好?

→　**B:** <u>秋天去北京最好不過了</u>。
<u>秋天去北京最好不过了</u>。

**1. A:** 張天明的母親覺得他念什麼合適?　　finance
张天明的母亲觉得他念什么合适?

**B:** _____ 。

**2. A:** 母親節快到了,送什麼禮物給媽媽好?　flowers
母亲节快到了,送什么礼物给妈妈好?

**B:** _____ 。

**3. A:** 下學期選什麼課輕鬆?　　　　　　　drawing
下学期选什么课轻松?

**B:** _____ 。

**F.** Connect the following individual sentences into a coherent narrative by adding connecting devices, deleting unnecessary pronouns, etc. (INTERPRETIVE AND PRESENTATIONAL)

1. 去年寒假我跟女朋友去中國旅行。
   去年寒假我跟女朋友去中国旅行。

2. 我們12月15號坐飛機去北京。
   我们12月15号坐飞机去北京。

3. 我們18號坐火車去哈爾濱。
   我们18号坐火车去哈尔滨。

4. 我們在哈爾濱看了冰燈，冰燈漂亮極了。
   我们在哈尔滨看了冰灯，冰灯漂亮极了。

5. 我們22號從哈爾濱一下子到了南方的廣州。
   我们22号从哈尔滨一下子到了南方的广州。

6. 廣州比哈爾濱暖和多了。
   广州比哈尔滨暖和多了。

7. 廣州有很多花，很漂亮。
   广州有很多花，很漂亮。

8. 我和女朋友24號回她南京老家。
   我和女朋友24号回她南京老家。

9. 女朋友的父母看見我好像很高興。
   女朋友的父母看见我好像很高兴。

10. 我們在女朋友家過了新年。
    我们在女朋友家过了新年。

11. 1月3號我們回到美國。
    1月3号我们回到美国。

**G.** Translate the following sentences into Chinese. (PRESENTATIONAL)

**1.** Chinese New Year is coming. There are beginning to be more people in shopping centers and restaurants.

_____

**2.** Professor Wang was very interested in this issue. As soon as he got home, he started to read up on the issue.

_____

**3.** Little Lin plans to go to graduate school after graduation, and doesn't plan to work.

_____

**4.** My father likes to eat spicy (things), and my mother likes to eat sweet (things).

_____

**H.** Translate the following dialogues into Chinese. (PRESENTATIONAL)

**1. A:** Are you busy next week?

_____

**B:** Monday, I'll have a piano lesson; Tuesday, I'll have a swimming lesson; Wednesday...

_____

**A:** OK, OK. It seems that you have a full schedule. Never mind, I'll ask someone else to dinner.

_____

**2. A:** Where would you like to travel this winter? Let's go to Harbin, OK?

_____

**B:** Harbin's ice lanterns are very famous, but it's too cold.

_____

**A:** Then let's go to the south, to Hainan (海南).

_____

**B:** Hainan is fun, but too many people go sightseeing there.

_____

**A:** How do you feel about going to Yunnan? It's neither too cold nor too hot, and there are not too many tourists.

_____

**B:** Many places in Yunnan are spring-like throughout the year. It's a great place to visit.

_____

**A:** So that means you agree to go to Yunnan?

_____

**B:** The only thing is it's too far away.

_____

**A:** Now I know: you are a traveler who likes to sit at home.

_____

**3. A:** Have you been to Nanjing? Is Nanjing a fun place?

_____

**B:** Yes, I have. Nanjing is a really fun place with a very long history. It's by the Yangtze River and has great natural conditions.

_____

**A:** What about the landscape?

_____

**B:** The landscape is very beautiful, too.

_____

**A:** Do you want to go to Nanjing again?

_____

**B:** Yes. My parents were born and grew up in Nanjing.

_____

**A:** Then let's go this summer.

_____

**B:** Nanjing is too hot in the summer. We'd better go in the spring or in the fall.

_____

**I.** Translate the passages into Chinese. (PRESENTATIONAL)

**1.** There are tall mountains as well as plateaus in Yunnan. Therefore, geographical conditions differ greatly. Everywhere the landscape is very beautiful. In many places, no matter when you go it's neither too cold nor too hot. It is very suitable for tourism.

_____

_____

_____

_____

_____

**2.** America's topography is very similar to China's. The latitude is almost the same, and so is the land area. However, the population is only a quarter (四分之一) of China's [population]. In American's southwest there are also tall mountains, plateaus, and deserts, and the landscape is beautiful. I hear that during holidays tourist sites are also crowded with people.

_____

_____

_____

_____

_____

**3.** The population of China's northeast is smaller than that of the coastal area. There is a big plain, and winter there is very cold. Harbin's ice lanterns are often mentioned on TV. That is why many people in China know about them.

_____

_____

_____

_____

_____

**J.** Do some research and complete the following sentences. Proper nouns can be written in English. If you like a challenge and don't mind a bit more work, then you can fill in the names in Chinese. (INTERPRETIVE AND PRESENTATIONAL)

1. 世界上最大的沙漠是
   世界上最大的沙漠是_____。

2. 世界上最高的山是_____。

3. 世界上最高的高原是_____。

4. 世界上最長的河流是
   世界上最长的河流是_____。

5. 世界上人口最多的國家(country)是
   世界上人口最多的国家(country)是_____。

6. 世界上緯度最北的國家是
   世界上纬度最北的国家是_____。

**K.** Write an introduction to your hometown or the place where you currently live. Include information such as its latitude and longitude, where it is located within the state or the country, whether there are mountains, rivers, plateaus, deserts, or plains nearby, and its population. (PRESENTATIONAL)

**L.** Choose either 四川, 新疆, 雲南/云南, or 廣東/广东 and write an introduction about it. Find out where it is located within China, what kind of topographical features it has, where its population is primarily concentrated, what the climate is like, what kind of cuisine it is famous for, etc. (PRESENTATIONAL)

## M. Storytelling (PRESENTATIONAL)

Write a story in Chinese based on the four cartoons below. Make sure that your story has a beginning, a middle, and an end. Also make sure that the transition from one picture to the next is smooth and logical.

1

2
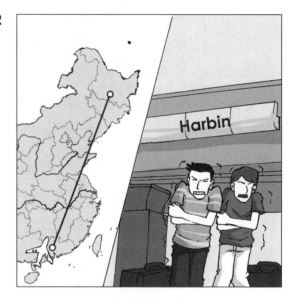

3

4

# Let's Review (LESSONS 6–10)

## I. How Good Is Your Pronunciation?

Write down the correct pronunciation and tones of the following short sentences in *pinyin*, and use a tape recorder or computer to record them. Hand in the recording to your teacher if asked. Then translate each sentence into English. (INTERPRETIVE)

**1.** 他們小兩口整天鬧彆扭。
他们小两口整天闹别扭。

_____

_____

**2.** 吵架解決不了問題。
吵架解决不了问题。

_____

_____

**3.** 説不定他們是真心相愛。
说不定他们是真心相爱。

_____

_____

**4.** 母親幾乎不看網絡新聞。
母亲几乎不看网络新闻。

_____

_____

5. 這個軟件已經落伍了。
   这个软件已经落伍了。

_____

_____

6. 結果他玩遊戲玩上癮了。
   结果他玩游戏玩上瘾了。

_____

_____

7. 她收入少，經濟負擔重。
   她收入少，经济负担重。

_____

_____

8. 花錢容易掙錢難。
   花钱容易挣钱难。

_____

_____

9. 農村孩子可以受到良好的教育。
   农村孩子可以受到良好的教育。

_____

_____

10. 她嫌打工影響學習。
    她嫌打工影响学习。

_____

_____

11. 她希望取得碩士和博士學位。
    她希望取得硕士和博士学位。

_____

_____

**12.** 家長應該尊重子女的選擇。
家长应该尊重子女的选择。

_____

_____

**13.** 旅行的路綫已經決定了。
旅行的路线已经决定了。

_____

_____

**14.** 沙漠中看不到河流。
沙漠中看不到河流。

_____

_____

**15.** 雲南有些地方四季如春。
云南有些地方四季如春。

_____

_____

## II. Put Your Chinese to Good Use! (PRESENTATIONAL)

Complete the following tasks in Chinese.

You are spending a semester in China and run into the following scenarios:

**A.** You have to set up a blind date for a Chinese friend. Who among your acquaintances would make a good match? Make a compatibility list.

_____

_____

_____

_____

_____

_____

_____

_____

**B.** You are an internet fanatic; how would you convince your friends how useful and helpful the internet can be for daily living? What reasons might be on your list?

_____

_____

_____

_____

_____

**C.** Your Chinese friends ask you to explain how American students finance their education. Write an outline for your talk.

**D.** You need to recruit some Chinese tutors for an American school. Prepare a flyer explaining the qualifications you are looking for.

**E.** You are asked to promote tourism for your hometown. Prepare a simple brochure describing the landscape and climate of your hometown.

_____

_____

_____

_____

_____

_____

_____

_____

## III. Getting to Know Yourself! (PRESENTATIONAL)

Make lists in Chinese.

**A.** How would you describe your personality traits? What do you like about yourself? What would you like to change about yourself?

| Positive | Negative |
|----------|----------|
| _____ | _____ |
| _____ | _____ |
| _____ | _____ |
| _____ | _____ |
| _____ | _____ |

**B.** Explain what you like and don't like about the internet.

Positive                                Negative

_____    _____

_____    _____

_____    _____

_____    _____

_____    _____

**C.** List some choices that you think could save money and those that could waste money.

Save money                              Waste money

_____    _____

_____    _____

_____    _____

_____    _____

_____    _____

**D.** List the things that you think a parent should and should not do to give a child a balanced childhood.

| Should do | Should not do |
| --- | --- |
| _____ | _____ |
| _____ | _____ |
| _____ | _____ |
| _____ | _____ |
| _____ | _____ |

**E.** List the things that would attract you to or deter you from visiting a tourist destination.

| Attract | Deter |
| --- | --- |
| _____ | _____ |
| _____ | _____ |
| _____ | _____ |
| _____ | _____ |
| _____ | _____ |

# IV. Express Yourself! (PRESENTATIONAL)

Based on, but not limited to, the information you have provided in Parts II and III, present an oral report or write a short essay in Chinese in response to each of the following questions.

**A.** Your friends are trying to find you a boyfriend or girlfriend. What would you tell them to ensure they find a good match for you?

**B.** You are asked to comment on the impact the internet has had on people's daily lives. What would you say?

**C.** You are asked to talk to high school and college students on how to live within their means and be financially responsible. What would you say?

**D.** You are an educator. What would be your advice to parents on how to give their children a happy childhood while preparing them for their future careers?

**E.** You are a tour guide planning to lead a one-month trip to China in the winter. What route would you choose, what places would you visit, and what do you need to know about those places?